Lifegiving *lights the path on how to be a lifegiving woman. It will be a lifegiver to every woman who reads it. Tammy's insights, stories, and Scripture are an encouragement to the soul.*

—Barbara Rainey, author of *A Mother's Legacy* and co-author of numerous books with her husband, Dennis

This message is long overdue and one the daughters and granddaughters of the feminist movement need to hear. This book has liberated me to be the lifegiving woman I was created to be.

—Lisa Ryan, author and co-host of The 700 Club

Lifegiving *is a rich and warm invitation to every woman who wants to experience life to fullness without exhausting herself. The book you hold has just what you need to change the atmosphere of your home into a garden of life, beauty and rejoicing. Prepare to be blessed, strengthened and encouraged.*

—Lisa Bevere, author of *Kissed the Girls and Made Them Cry*

This book is a passionate charge to women to let the love and life God has placed within them flow unrestrained from their hearts to those around them.

—Pastor Ted and Gayle Haggard, New Life Church Colorado Springs, CO, author of *Primary Purpose, The Lifegiving Church* and *Letters from Home*

Like a delectable, triple chocolate cake, Lifegiving *is layered with rich biblical teaching, poignant true stories, and topped with sumptuous creative ideas. Tammy's effervescent personality sparkles from every page. Allow her to take your hand and lead you to a place of breathtaking beauty as she shows you how to find majesty in the mundane and splendor in the commonplace.*

—Lorraine Pintus, author of *Intimate Issues* with Linda Dillow

Lifegiving *is a breath of life and the snapshot of a transparent woman who has touched the heart of God and the people around her.*

—Coral Kennedy, co-founder and co-pastor, The North Church, Carrollton, TX and co-president of Church on the Rock International

Lifegiving

Discovering the Secrets to a Beautiful Life

Tammy Maltby

with Tamra Farah

MOODY PUBLISHERS
CHICAGO

Unless otherwise indicated, all Scripture quotations are taken from the *Holy Bible, New International Version*®. NIV ®. Copyright © 1973, 1978, 1984 by International Bible Society. Used by permission of Zondervan Publishing House. All rights reserved.

Scripture quotations marked NCV are taken from New Century Version ®, copyright ©1987, 1988, 1991 by Word Publishing, a division of Thomas Nelson, Inc. Used by permission.

Scripture quotations marked NLT are taken from *The Holy Bible, New Living Translation*, copyright © 1996. Used by permission of Tyndale House Publishers, Inc., Wheaton, Illinois 60189. All rights reserved.

Scripture quotations marked NKJV are taken from the *New King James Version*. Copyright © 1982 by Thomas Nelson, Inc. Used by permission. All rights reserved.

Produced with the assistance of The Livingstone Corporation. Project staff includes Paige Drygas, Neil Wilson, Ashley Taylor, Greg Longbons, and Kirk Luttrell. Interior design by Mark Wainwright.

Library of Congress Cataloging-in-Publication Data

Maltby, Tammy.
    Lifegiving : discovering the secrets to a beautiful life / Tammy Maltby with Tamra Farah.
        p. cm.
    Includes bibliographical references.
    ISBN 0-8024-1360-9
    1. Christian women--Religious life. I. Farah, Tamra. II. Title.

BV 4527 .M24 2002
248.8'43--dc21

2002075385

1 3 5 7 9 10 8 6 4 2

Printed in the United States of America

Tammy

To my lifegiving mother, Ramona Hanson:
You have taught me to live a beautiful life.
You have daily mentored the breathtaking mystery and
beautiful pleasure of giving your life away.
How could I thank you enough?
How could I love you more?
You are a treasure among ten thousand.

To my lifegiving daughters, Mackenzie Rachel, Tatiana
Rebekah, Mikia Joy:
You are the most beautiful of all lifegiving women to me . . .
yet mere words could not accurately paint a picture of the
beauty I see in you.
My daughters, be courageous, love hard, dance freely.
You were created for this day, this hour, to be God's
promise keepers to a lost and dying world.
Press in . . . never pull back . . . live a life of love . . .

Tamra

To the bouquet of lifegivers who have fragranced my life
along the way . . . some were annual, others are perennial. I
dedicate this book to you, for your lifegiving lifestyles have
trained mine, as I hope mine will train my daughter's. For
my mothers, Barbara and Barbara and JoAnne, and my
friends Marilyn, Phyllis, Marky, Gayle, Becky, Mary, and
Melody. I would not be me without you.

contents

part 1

THE SECRET LIFE OF THE LIFEGIVER

part 2

THE LIFEGIVING LIFESTYLE

part 3

A FEW GOOD LIFEGIVERS

acknowledgments

A heartfelt thanks from Tammy to . . .

My husband, Butch.

How do I begin to thank you for all you have done to make this dream come true? You encouraged, loved, forgave, and strengthened me. Not to mention fulfilling my request to read my copy just "one more time." I have never known a man like you, Butch. You are the most gifted, strong, enduring example of a real man out there. I love your passion, your tenderness, your love for me and the children. Thank you for taking this life journey with me. . . . I'd do it all over again.

"All my soul follows you, love . . . and I live in being yours." (Robert Browning)

My wonderful son, Samuel.

If you grow to be half the man that you have been as a boy, the world will be rich indeed. Thank you, Sam, for running me hot baths, for backrubs and crazy jokes. You delight my heart . . . completely. God lovingly knew you would be the perfect son for us. I adore you, strong knight.

My parents, Ken and Ramona.

Thank you, Mom and Dad, for raising me in a godly family and staying true to the Lord through so many years. Thank you mostly for loving me and believing that my life would somehow be restored. Look what God has done!

The Hawaii Five-O women.

Maryjo Valder, Jennifer Peters, Lynn Brown, and Lisa Bevere, you are the most fun women . . . ever! I love the fifty-five years of combined friendship. Thank you for loving and living well. Oh baby . . . fifty, here we come! It will be beautiful.

My cocreator, Tamra.

What a mind you have, girl. I love everything you brought to this project. Thank you for helping me bring it all alive . . . in living color, no less! You are a gift to me.

My prayer warrior, Lorraine Pintus.

Girl, I just love you. Thank you for passionately giving me life.

My friend Bill Jensen.

Years ago you saw it. Thanks for telling me over and over again. Encouragement is a powerful tool.

My friends at Moody Publishers.

Greg Thornton, Elsa Mazon, and Bill Thrasher. Thank you for believing so strongly in this message. Working with you has been the most wonderful process, abundantly beyond my wildest dreams. Thank you. Thank you.

Paige Drygas.

Your excellent editorial skills fine-tuned this running thing! You have so much to look forward to. Even as a young woman, God has made your life a picture of loveliness.

My dearest Friend and Lover of my soul, Jesus, my ultimate Lifegiver.

This is but a small attempt to reflect the mercy and beauty You have given me. When I was in a far-off land You came running and clothed me with forgiveness and adorned me with compassion. *You are so beautiful to me.* Oh, to gaze upon Your face. Oh, to know You. I pour it out, Lord, that You would be pleased. Make it something beautiful for You.

A heartfelt thanks from Tamra . . .

I am thankful for my husband, Barry, who has given me an incredible life these nineteen years and has cheered me on in this writing project. His kindness, love, faithfulness, generosity, strength, ingenuity, and passion are my daily comfort and joy.

My gratitude goes to my faithful and dear friends Gayle Haggard, Phyllis Stanley, and Marky Gilbert, who bring so much life to me. And they know the secrets for living beautifully.

I thank God for our local church, New Life, where lifegiving is a wonderful part of the culture. I have such a love and deep appreciation for all the precious women I have had the privilege of walking with here over the years.

For all of our friends at Moody Publishers, Livingstone, and Journey who have been kind and creative, I am grateful. Tammy and I are blessed.

And I would like to thank my loving friend Tammy Maltby for asking me to help her write this book, the pages of which are heavy laden with our mutual passion.

A special letter for you . . .

My dear friend,

Have you ever considered that there are secrets to living a beautiful life? These secrets await your discovery in this book.

Will you step with me into the glorious *secret place of the lifegiver?* It's a mysterious place that offers understanding for the ache of your heart, peaceful rest for your weary soul, and breathtaking beauty to give you strength to carry on.

A place you were created for . . . a beautiful, lifegiving place. Friend, this is the dwelling your heart longs for, aches for, though you may think it only a dream. . . . It's a bountiful life that calls you, beckons you, summons you by name to come and sup a while . . . to drink deeply from the well of refreshment. It is a peaceful place free of encumbrances, where you'll discover satisfaction, freedom, and a renewed purpose for living.

Nearly twelve years ago I set out on this life-changing journey. Beginning in the barren wilderness of my broken and desperate heart, I ventured into the *secret places* of a lifegiving woman. Unbeknownst to me, this journey would touch my heart's desire, provide unmistakably clear vision, and present the rhythms of love that brought me into the dance of my life.

You see, lifegiving is a *beautiful way of life*. It's the magnificent discovery of God's loving fingerprints in the clay of everyday living. It is beauty seen in the mundane, splendor experienced in the commonplace. It is a mind-set, a lifestyle, and a magnificent life-changing touch. Simply put, you were created *in* beauty and *for* beauty, and your soul will find its truest purpose in the unseen acts of love and servanthood that are lifegiving.

Sound intriguing?

Come take a stroll with me into the life of beauty and strength. Friend, here I want to introduce you to the power of the ultimate Lifegiver, Jesus, who alone can refresh your soul and offer the contentment you so desperately long for. In this place I yearn to take off my makeup and greet you with the honest musing of a woman who, like you, is a work in progress. I have known the diversions of sin along the road and the painful consequences of waywardness. But I have also known the healing touch of the Master, and I will never be the same.

Discover with me how lifegiving is much more than an idea—

It's a breathtaking, beautiful way to live and love.
Your life will never be the same. . . .

Warmly,
Tammy Maltby

part one

The Secret Life of
the Lifegiver

secret life

chapter one

Lifegivers Are Beautiful

beautiful

Success has nothing to
do with what you gain in
life or accomplish for
yourself. Success is what
you do for others.

Danny Thomas

What does a lifegiving woman look like?

Several weeks ago I entered a place and was immediately met with the warmth of a lifegiving woman. There was ease about her, a quiet confidence and an undeniable inner strength. Many others were there when I arrived, greeting and sharing with one another. Some even extended a thoughtful welcome. But when this lifegiving woman reached out, I was *deeply touched.* She embraced my heart; she lifted my spirit and refreshed me. There was tangible love, enthusiastic energy, passion, and grace in her presence. As I moved past her, I realized that I felt nurtured, cared for, and valued. It was as if I had strolled past a lovely garden. I longed to linger in the presence of this woman who knew the secret of lifegiving, to breathe in the sweet fragrance of such simple yet transforming beauty. In a brief encounter, she gave me life.

How will you know when you have met a lifegiving woman?

Well, it goes something like this.

When she speaks, you do not go away licking your wounds from a hurtful word. Instead, even her everyday words seem to be infused with lifegiving power and encouragement.

When she does a good deed, you do not feel the heavy weight of obligation to return the favor. Instead, you are inspired to do something lovely in return.

When she is with you, you never feel a cold shoulder, because she brings warmth and acceptance into your life.

When you go to her home for a meal, you don't feel impressed by the expensive décor (even if she does have a big budget!). Instead, you feel the warmth of her home and the comfort of the beauty you find there.

When you are around her, you don't feel overwhelmed by who she is. Instead, you feel inspired to be who you were meant to be.

When you walk away from her, you don't feel discouraged by her accomplishments compared to yours. Instead, you walk away motivated to do what you never thought possible.

Do you know a lifegiving woman?

If you do, then you understand that she has brought love and warmth into your life. She has inspired you to do what you never thought possible. She has encouraged you to reach out and take risks. She has refreshed you with living water when the well of your life has run dry.

I know when I have been with a lifegiving woman, because whether she has shared a word or a deed, I am helped, encouraged, and deeply inspired.

How easy it is for one benevolent being to diffuse pleasure around him. And how truly is a kind heart a fountain of gladness, making everything in its vicinity to freshen into smiles. Washington Irving

Many reach out to us, but only a few reach far enough to touch our very hearts. What is the difference?

The difference is found in the ancient secrets of lifegiving.

Ordinary women give extraordinary life

I heard a beautiful story of a lifegiving woman who lived in New York City. On a very cold December day, a little boy stood barefoot before a shoe store, peering through the window, shivering in the cold. A woman approached the boy and said, "My little fellow, why are you looking so earnestly in that window?"

"I was asking God to give me a pair of shoes," was the boy's reply.

The woman took him by the hand and went into the store. She asked the clerk to get half a dozen pairs of socks for the boy. She then asked if he could give her a basin of water and a towel. He quickly brought them to her. She took the boy to the back part of the store, removed her gloves, knelt down, and washed and dried his little feet. By this time the clerk had returned with the socks. She placed a pair upon the boy's feet and then purchased him a pair of shoes. She tied up the remaining pairs of socks and gave them to him, patted him on the head, and said, "No doubt, my little fellow, you feel more comfortable now."

As she turned to go, the astonished boy caught her by the hand, and looking up in her face with tears in his eyes, he asked, "Are you God's wife?"

Think of it! Her simple act of lifegiving caused him to wonder if she was God's own bride!

Restorative, lifegiving actions are being acted out daily by ordinary women. Their actions and words may seem simple, but they have found the secret to living a beautiful life.

Cohosting the television program *Aspiring Women* has given me wonderful opportunities to meet remarkable, everyday, lifegiving women. Linda Lampeth is one such woman. You may never see her face on the news or her name in national headlines, but she is a true lifegiver.

Linda was living in a small community in Texas with her husband, her two girls, and her baby boy when challenging circumstances began to unfold. Due to medical mistreatment, her little boy, Ronnie, became deaf.

Linda knew she had to make some very difficult decisions. A very optimistic woman, she was determined that her son would learn to function in a hearing world. As Ronnie entered kindergarten, he seemed to be on target with his scholastic development. But by third grade, her son was falling further and further behind. Endless hours were spent each evening just trying to catch up on all the information he had missed during the day. Something had to change.

Linda was about to lay down her life—her agenda, her plans, her schedule—to give life to her son.

One sunny Texas morning, Linda boarded a bright yellow school bus and went to the fourth grade with her deaf son. Yes, she became a part of the class. With her little son facing her, she slowly spoke every word as Ronnie read her lips. Finding that Ronnie was quickly progressing in school with her help, Linda continued throughout that year to be her son's ears. And then she continued the next year, and the next year, and so on.

> It is the glow within that creates beauty. People are like stained-glass windows. They sparkle like crystal in the sun. At night they continue to sparkle only if there is light from within. Bonnie Green

Every day. Every class. Every grade. Linda even attended high school with her son and helped him graduate with honors. She proudly walked with all the seniors to receive her own diploma!

The most remarkable part of this story is that many years later when cochlear implants were developed, Ronnie was eligible to receive the treatment due to the fact that he had learned to speak and lip-read at a young age. If he had only learned to sign, his brain would have been unable to receive the stimulus needed to actually begin hearing again. The medical miracle of cochlear implants has allowed Ronnie to receive 90 percent of his hearing back! This all began when one lifegiving mother made a commitment to sacrifice herself every day as an offering of love.

This is the everyday glory of a lifegiving woman.

Many famous lifegivers have impacted their families, communities, and even the world down through the ages—women like Clara Barton, founder of the American Red Cross; Golda Meir, Prime

Minister of Israel when the fledgling nation needed strong leadership; or Mother Hale, an African-American grandmother who founded the largest ministry to crack babies in New York City. These women brought life to lifeless situations. They were bearers of hope in seemingly hopeless situations. They infused life into everyone who touched them. They refused to allow circumstances to cloud their vision. They took painful risks to give life.

Life in the face of death

One unmistakable lifegiver in modern times was Mother Teresa of Calcutta. Certainly we have all seen countless photographs of this small, frail woman clad in a nun's garb. Have you ever considered her a beautiful woman? Not by worldly standards. She wore no jewels, no makeup. Yet her life revealed an unmatched beauty that the entire world recognizes.

Few of us will pack our bags and move to the streets of Calcutta to minister to the dying like the Sisters of Charity. But all of us can glean qualities expressed by this small yet mighty lifegiver. Mother Teresa was more than an icon. She was a woman who flowed in the lifegiving nature given to her by God. This four-foot-eleven-inch nun sowed life with abandon!

Her example as a lifegiver is revealed in the book *No Greater Love*:

> In twenty-five years, we have picked up more than thirty-six thousand people from the streets and more than eighteen thousand have died a most beautiful death.
>
> When we pick them up from the street we give them a plate of rice. In no time we revive them. A few nights ago we picked up four people. One was

in a most terrible condition, covered with wounds,
full of maggots. I told the sisters I would take care
of her while they attended to the other three. *I really did all that my love could do for her.* I put her in
bed and then she took hold of my hand. She had
such a beautiful smile on her face and she said only,
"Thank you." Then she died.

There was a greatness of love. She was hungry
for love, and she received that love before she died.
She spoke only two words, but her understanding of
love was expressed in those two words.[1]

Even in horrific circumstances, Mother Teresa's lifegiving service
shone through. She knew the mystery of a beautiful death. She understood that even when a situation seemed impossible, the crisis
brought an opportunity for a life offering that was precious and
powerful.

In my mind, the most feminine woman is one with an eye and ear
for others and a heart for God. Emily Barns

I saw a glimpse of this Calcutta picture when traveling to Central
and South America to escort adopted babies to waiting families in the
United States. On one trip with a dear friend, Ruth, I encountered the
squalor of an orphanage where children battled for life daily. The
rooms were dark. The cribs were crowded. Diapers were soiled.
Death hung like a low moon in the sky.

I felt overwhelmed with the picture of pain before me. The natural question—*why?*—turned into anger and despair. At one point I
ran out of this "dying room," sobbing uncontrollably. I was too overwhelmed to stay in the presence of these infants who were barely

hanging on to life. Their desperate pain seemed so senseless, their hope so undeniably lost. I sat outside the door, sobbing and alone for some time.

Moments later, I sensed someone beside me, slowly closing in. It was my friend Ruth. She took my hand, and I heard her say softly, "Are you done?"

"Done with what?" I struggled to say.

"Done crying?" I wondered about the inappropriateness of the question. Couldn't she see the need? The dying? Couldn't she see that these little helpless lives were without hope?

With the resolve of a lifegiver, Ruth whispered, "Tammy, when you are finished crying, we can go and do something about it." In that moment I realized that my focus was on the pain of the situation, but her focus was on the lifegiving opportunity.

> You are certainly one of the joys of life for all who have ever come within a mile of you. Thomas Merton

You see, the lifegiver feels the pain but remembers that there is eternal currency to appropriate from the Father, like hope, love, peace, and life. His lifegiving bank is full to overflowing! We can write as many checks as we need for any amount we want. We can change the life of one, and then another and another. He only requires our trust and obedience.

How can I be a beautiful lifegiver?

Some of you may wonder, *Can I really be a woman like this? How do these lifegivers find passion to give to others when their lives abound with big demands on their limited time? Can I really live a beautiful life?* It may seem intimidating, even impossible, to most of you. Some of you harried wives and mothers may feel like you cannot even think about giving out beyond your own life's demands. Others of you may be single and feel your own needs are never met, let alone finding energy to meet the needs of others.

Many of us have never envisioned ourselves as lifegivers. We are overwhelmed with the pain that life has dealt us. Some of us have felt stirrings to be lifegivers but do not have the energy or the motivation to express this God-given capacity. Others of us may feel trapped by the mountain of tasks we face every day. We wonder, *How can I give a cup of cold water when I desperately need a drink? My need for personal refreshment is so great; how can I refresh another?*

Before we answer these questions, let's go back to the beginning. The very beginning, where lifegiving began . . . back in the garden. Yes, the very first garden—beautiful Eden! Friend, here we will discover why we have such a longing to give life.

chapter two

Lifegiving Began in a Garden

garden

In today's world . . . it is
still woman's business
to make life better, to
make tomorrow better
than today.

Helen Thames Raley

Given a choice, every woman would rather begin life in a beautiful garden than a barren wilderness. God would agree and thus chose to begin the incredible human drama of womanhood in a garden. Undoubtedly, God Almighty had many amazing places from which to choose. Yet He chose a garden to establish lifegiving—the magnificent Garden of Eden!

Adam, the very first human, was taken from the dust of the ground and was made from mud out in the wilderness. Genesis 2:7 gives the account: "The LORD God formed the man from the dust of the ground and breathed into his nostrils the breath of life, and the man became a living being." Clearly, that explains why men don't mind being dirty or sleeping out under the stars with stone pillows! As the mother of a son who loves the great outdoors, I understand this well. (Sister, the only thing that appeals to me about camping is all those cute hiking outfits—you know, the ones that make you *look* like you know what you're doing! Once the hot dogs are done roasting, give me a warm soft bed!)

After God made Adam, He let him discover for himself that there was no other created thing among all the creatures he had named that would be a good companion. But God had a plan! He had something in mind. This last creation would not come from the "dust of the ground"; rather, she would come from the most magnificent of all creation, God's best thus far—man himself.

But before God made this perfect helpmate for Adam, He planted a lifegiving garden. There in the secure confines of Eden, God fashioned a woman. The Master Gardener refined the body and form of the man and created something entirely new, something inspiring, something lovely, something of great beauty. Lifegiving began in an exquisite garden.

God chose to create us in the midst of loveliness and life, which *garden*

explains why a love of beauty is such a part of our identity as women. It resonates with our very being. As women, we have always longed to create and nurture places of beauty. We were designed for lifegiving.

This quest to beautify is reflected by women in every age and culture. Pick up a *National Geographic,* and you will see women from all over the world expressing their own unique versions of beauty. Whether their bronzed necks are draped with bones or shells or their white pillar necks are adorned with sparkling gems, you can tell that we women love beauty!

Back to the story. After looking at the woman, Adam decided on a name for his wondrous new companion. In Genesis 3:20, Adam called his wife "Eve," which means "life," for she would be the "mother of all the living."

Eve, the lifegiving woman! Eve, the first lifegiver, began her life in a picturesque garden. But her life wasn't without its problems.

In recent years we have been obsessed with figuring out what a woman should be allowed to do. God says in His Word a woman can do anything: the point is not what she does but what she is. Anne Ortlund

Where has all the beauty gone?

How many of you are already thinking, "Me, a beautiful, lifegiving woman? Impossible!" At this point you may feel your life looks more like the desert wasteland Adam was formed in than the beautiful garden in which Eve was fashioned. Some of us have faced a deteriorating marriage, a strained relationship with a parent, a consuming fear of inadequacy, and pangs of worthlessness as a mother or friend. Quiet demons may be whispering death to us in our personal and public lives. Some of us have experienced painful loss or emotional or physical abuse. We have all winced at our own hurtful words and attitudes that seem to cancel our potential as lifegivers. We wonder if being a true lifegiver is really possible.

While we know the stirrings of the lifegiver—we have the thought to reach out to a family member, write a letter to a friend, invite a lonely woman over for lunch, or take a meal to someone who is hurting—we don't seem to have the ability to actually *do* these life-giving things. Why can't we function like the lifegivers we were created to be?

We agonizingly look at other women who seem to flow in the river of life, loving and nurturing everyone they meet. We long to be in that river, but we do not know how to get from the desert wasteland of our own souls into the river of all lifegiving. Intimidation and rejection keep us captive.

Friend, there is hope for a radical transformation!

You see, it is precisely when our experience seems hopeless that eternal hope can be found. In this place of pain and weakness, we can tap into the reservoir of Christ's forgiveness. Has sin—yours or the sins of others against you—left you feeling like a sun-scorched prairie instead of a lush tropical forest? I want you to know that God can bring magnificent blooms in the driest desert of your life. The worst experiences of your life actually have the most lifegiving potential! I bet you never thought that could be possible.

I know I didn't.

My early twenties proved to be a time of great sorrow and significant personal failure. In this barren winter of my life, my heart was deeply wounded. By the time I was twenty-three years old, I knew the bitter taste of divorce. I had chosen to walk a false way that left me feeling contaminated and greatly distressed. The pain of this time was great, but the fallout effect was even greater. The debris found its home in the lives of so many who knew me.

During that season, I withdrew from most of my friends and family. The personal shame and disgrace seemed too great to bear. It was a lonely journey that took me further than I ever thought possible. I wore lifelessness and decay around me like a heavy cloak. The depression, hopelessness, and fear made my soul a desert wasteland. Worse yet, some of those who loved me were caused to question God's ways.

Personal failure is never easy, though I would venture to guess it has affected many of our personal lives. We long to have meaningful relationships, marriages, and friendships, only to find ourselves at the mercy of our own sinfulness or the sinfulness of others. The powerful venom of sin seeps into us and infects those around us.

I have always found it interesting that we can have scores of personal triumphs and trophies, academic crowns, and financial success and yet find ourselves in situations of emptiness and despair. So it was with my life. By all standards I had everything going for me. I grew up in a Christian family, went to a Christian college, had Christian friends. I did well in school, beauty pageants, and modeling and knew how to make a good impression. But all this success blinded me to my utter need for redemption. Never had I dealt with my own sinfulness and personal need. Then my failed marriage sent me headfirst into a desperate state of need. Thank God.

Paradise found!

In my brokenness, I began to see who God really is. I began to know Him as my loving Father, and I learned that in His great love, He would walk with me through my darkest valley of shame. He showed me how to break the powerful death grip that sin and selfishness had over my life. He gave me the courage to go to the deepest places of pain and find healing.

And herein lies the profound mystery of the lifegiving gospel of Christ: When we mourn, repent, and die to sin, we come to see our need for total dependence on God. This dependence frees us from the devastation of sin and creates a new place that God longs to reveal to us. In this beautiful, satisfying place, we have freedom over our wills and the circumstances that have held us in quiet desperation. Here we tap into lifegiving waters. Here we trade beauty for ashes, hope for despair. In Him we are forever changed and need never go back to that barren wasteland again.

Whatever is true, whatever is noble, whatever is right, whatever is pure, whatever is lovely, whatever is admirable—if anything is excellent or praiseworthy—think about such things. Philippians 4:8

If you are roaming in the wilderness of hurt, woundedness, damaged emotions, rejection, and bitterness, reach out! There is a Deliverer, a Healer for our souls. He wants to bring rivers of living water in the desert places in your life (Isaiah 41:17–18). He wants to bring you into the abundant life that Jesus promised.

We are not just being saved from sin and death; we are being translated into the kingdom of life! We do not merely have to survive; we can *live!* And as we receive life, we can then in turn pour life into those around us. We can begin to be the lifegivers we were created to be.

The trampled garden

Our sins and the sins of others against us are not the only deathblow to our lifegiving. Our culture has also sent us a clear message to suppress our tendency for lifegiving. For the last thirty years, women have heard the message, "You can have it all!" When we were young, this used to sound like a cheer from the sidelines on the road of life.

Now, overwhelmed and in over our heads, it sounds more like a death knell! Many women have stretched themselves to have it all, only to find they have nothing left to give.

The lifestyle mapped out for us by the radical feminists of the 1960s has stirred up conflict in women's souls. In *What Our Mothers Didn't Tell Us,* Danielle Crittenden assesses where women are now, after three decades of being told to put their personal goals above home and family. She observes that many married women today feel a sort of unfairness about the inner conflict between their personal goals and the urge to fulfill the needs of their loved ones. She says this urge "does not just extend to what her husband or the society around her expects her to do but, more subtly, to her *own* impulse to do things and make sacrifices for her husband and family."[2]

> The aim of life is to spend it for something that will outlast it.
> William James

Many women have unwittingly thought this impulse to serve their families was something to be managed or even snuffed out. Radical feminist Gloria Steinem called the impulse in women to make sacrifices for others—to nurture and care for—a "compassion disease." Though feminist teachings tried to nail shut the coffin on the lifegiving part of our feminine nature, no one checked to see if it was really dead. The lifegiving nature of three generations of women may have been buried alive, but the impulse and deep desire to be lifegivers is indelibly stamped upon our natures by God. This aspect of our feminine nature is too powerful to simply *die*. It is just desperately gasping for air and longing for the light of day.

Many women today are at war within themselves. The battlefield is our souls, and the casualties are often our marriages, children, and even our culture. If women are not caretakers, then who will be? If women stop nurturing, who will pick up the slack? If women do not begin compassionate social movements, who will?

It is good that women now enjoy respect as doctors, lawyers, pilots, writers, executives, entrepreneurs, and a full range of vocations. Yet many have discovered that being chained to a desk in an office is not much different than being chained to the kitchen sink. The issue today is whether we—in the process of pursuing respect in the marketplace—have lost something in our identity as women. Have we suppressed our God-designed nature as lifegivers somewhere along the way?

True to our nature

As lifegiving women, we are uniquely designed to enrich the lives of those around us. We can bring warmth, love, nurture, and grace that are often missing in the corporate world or our individual worlds. Which is more valuable—opening the top of the copier and sliding in a report or opening the oven door and sliding in a cookie sheet? None of us want the mother of a toddler who is home baking cookies to feel that her work is less valuable than that of the woman working in an office. For nearly three generations, we have heard messages from movies, sitcoms, advertisements, and women's magazines about finding our value in work outside the home. Still, a majority of women today—if they believed they had a choice—would rather stay home with their preschool-aged children than work. Yet very few do it without a great inner conflict over their perceived sense of self-worth.

A few years ago, a TV panel of accomplished career women mused over some intangible quality that they have noticed is missing from their lives. Finally they put their finger on it: No one is engaged in the day-to-day lifegiving activities that warm our hearts and feed our souls. They seemed to ask, "Who is making homemade *anything?*

Who is bringing fresh flowers, lighting candles for the family to enjoy, thinking about the extra touches, the seemingly insignificant lifegiving activities that nurture and nourish, that create warmth and security at home and in society?"

Friend, we can win the battle in our souls and be the lifegivers we were meant to be, enriching the lives of all those around us. It is time to resuscitate this powerful facet of our natures by embracing the lifestyle of the lifegiver. It is time to reaffirm in one another what has always been true but has often been suppressed. It is time to rediscover our full capacity as lifegivers and live the abundant life that Jesus came to give us.

A bird does not sing because it has an answer. It sings because it has a song. Chinese Proverb

---

Do lifegivers wake up with a smile every day like Beaver Cleaver's mom, don a freshly starched white apron, and flip flapjacks for the family in pumps and pearls? Of course not. This uncorking of our lifegiving nature does not mean we will now, in unison, arise each morning without bed-head and bad breath. As our natural bent to nurture, care for, and give is called to life, it will not be the end of irritation with kids who perpetually leave their dirty clothes on the floor or teenagers who speak hurtful words. We are not proposing a panacea of lifegiving or recruiting a few good lifegivers to march in Stepford-wife unison, with plastic smiles outlined in red lipstick, vacuum in one hand and freshly baked pie in the other. But, yes, we are proposing that we take the time to see the value of creating many aspects of beauty in our lives. It is time to reach out and have our neighbors— real, not virtual—in for a cup of tea so that we can speak life into their desperate moments.

The lifegiving aspect of our femininity is not composed of lace, curls, pumps, and pearls. It is multifaceted. Lifegiving requires an inner core of strength, because it is not easy to keep giving when no one gives back. It requires wisdom, a stout heart, decisiveness, and an eye for beauty. Women committed to developing and expressing the lifegiving aspect of their natures, who embrace the value of their drive to nurture and nourish life around them, are compassionate, caring, thoughtful, and creative. A lifegiving lifestyle is not for the faint of heart.

Like the flower that pushes its way up through the cracks in the sidewalk, we ultimately cannot suppress this essential and powerful aspect of our nature as women. We were designed to give life!

In the midst of such confusing messages, there is still hope for our trampled, lifegiving gardens. We are not lifegivers because we have mastered the art of servanthood or because we have outgoing personalities. Simply put, we are lifegivers by design. God Himself fashioned us to be lifegivers. It is a great urge within each one of us to nourish and nurture life around us. This powerful potential in every woman is unleashed in Christ, the Ultimate Lifegiver.

chapter three

The Power of the Seed

power

Surprise me, Lord, as a

seed surprises itself....

George Herbert

All beautiful gardens start with good, rich soil. The soil is the first and most foundational element. To plant seeds, to see them mature and bring forth fruit, and eventually to see the new seed come forth from the mature plants, we must first start with good soil. Good soil, along with proper conditions for the best possible growth, gives promise for a beautiful, lifegiving garden.

As in all successful gardens, lifegiving begins with the soil of our lives. Having good soil means we have the nutrients within our own souls to provide adequate support for lifegiving. In adding these proper nutrients to the soil, we give the seed the best chance for growth. This garden becomes a place where others can put down roots that will help them absorb the lifegiving elements so vital for healthy development.

So what does that really look like? How can we prepare ourselves to be a lifegiving garden?

A good gardener must properly prepare the soil. If we were to go out in our own backyards and put seed in the dirt, most likely that dirt would not have the proper balance of nutrients to support the seed and bring forth the mature plant (especially where I live in Colorado, where the soil is sand and clay!). We need to add the proper nutrients to the soil for best possible growth of the seed. What are the nutrients we need in the soil of our lives?

First, we must spend time with Jesus.
We must know Christ. What does He look like? What is His character? We must begin to see with spiritual eyes what He would do in any situation. A lifestyle of lifegiving is really all about Him, His character, and His ways. Christ Himself is our role model of abundant and costly lifegiving.

Second, we must enrich the soil of our lives in prayer.

Prayer is so much more than just talking to God. It is also the Holy Spirit's speaking to us and for us and moving us to share our thoughts, concerns, and thanksgiving with Him. Prayer is a reflection of the mysteries of life from the highest point of view. Ralph Herring said, "You can accomplish more in one hour with God than in a lifetime without Him. Prayer is a summit meeting in the very throne room of the universe. There is no higher level." Prayer is the power source. It is the fertilizer in the garden of our lives producing a "Miracle Gro" experience! It boosts the lifegiving potential within us.

Whoever lives true life will love true love. Elizabeth Barrett Browning

---

Third, we must submit ourselves to the deep inner work of the Word of God.

When we allow God's Word to have free reign in our hearts and minds, it will reveal to us life-draining parasites that keep us from giving our lives away in meaningful ways. Things like selfishness, control, unrealistic expectations, shame, and rejection drain our lifegiving potential. As we lay those things at the foot of the cross, Christ can then bring the resurrection power of His life into our lives.

Life out of death: the story of compost

This brings us to the story of the compost. Successful gardeners know a dramatic enrichment of the soil occurs when it has been tilled with compost. Compost is actually composed of things that once had life but now are dead. As the once-living material of compost decomposes, it produces qualities that will later enrich the soil of the garden. It makes soil out of dirt. In the same way, it is the death of our own sin and the sins of others against us that will ultimately produce life within us.

These dead things in the hand of a loving master gardener actually become the most sought after and valued additives to a lifegiving garden. The Holy Spirit faithfully tills these dead things into our lifegiving garden, and in doing so He creates a place of beauty and depth. In this process of death to self, the life-changing power of God flows from us to those around us. God's power is best seen in the lifeless graveyards of our own personal shame and sin. This is the secret and powerful exchange necessary to become lifegivers. We go from life to death to real life again.

> We pardon in the degree that we love. Francois La Rochefoucauld

The story of the sinful woman in Luke 7:36–50 is the story of such compost. Here is a woman who carried death and decay around her like tattered garments. Yet Christ's love transformed the tattered garments into a royal gown. In fact, her great need for forgiveness unleashed the power of Christ in her life to become royalty in His kingdom.

This is undoubtedly my favorite story of the lifegiving power of Jesus. Christ's encounter with the sinful and shame-ridden woman and the impact of His transforming words should give us all hope of transformation. Here we see how Jesus, the ultimate Lifegiver, gave life in exchange for the dead places offered to Him.

The Known Woman

Jesus had been invited to dine at the home of a Pharisee. Throughout the Gospels, we see the Pharisees set out to entrap, ensnare, and rebuke all who were less than what they deemed righteous. Jesus was no exception. As the bantering and questioning darted around the dinner table, a known sinful woman entered the house.

Imagine, if you will, the fearful yet exhilarating moment. She had a reputation. The Bible calls her a prostitute. She was known by all, loved by none. This outcast woman had lost so much and needed so much. Shame and rejection must have been her only constant companions.

Surely she had heard Jesus preach, and in repentance she was determined and desperate to lead a new life. This outcast of society, this used-up and thrown-out woman, knew Jesus was her only hope— if she could just see Him, touch Him, and experience Him. Yet she was very aware that to embrace such forgiveness and hope she first had to face the harshest, most judgmental men of the day, the Pharisees, men who perhaps paid her by night and shunned her by day.

Even so, the longing for true life and restoration compelled her to seek out the true Giver of all life. She was desperate to see this man Jesus, a man so different than all the others she had known. He promised forgiveness for sin, and oh yes, she was well aware of her sin. He came to give and bless, not take and shame.

He said He was the Life.

The great Redeemer, Jesus of Galilee, was so wonderfully, terrifyingly close.

Forget the former things; do not dwell on the past. See, I am doing a new thing! Now it springs up; do you not perceive it? I am making a way in the desert and streams in the wasteland. Isaiah 43:18–19

I can imagine that as she entered the room grunts of rejection and horror greeted her. Voices fell silent. All eyes glared in judgment. As this broken woman pushed through her shame to reach out to the Giver of all true life, "she stood behind him at his feet weeping, she began to wet his feet with her tears. Then she wiped them with her hair, kissed them and poured perfume on them" (Luke 7:38).

This is a picture of complete humility. No words were spoken—only salty tears falling ever so slowly onto the Master's feet. He submitted to her gesture of love and honor. Can you picture the depth of her emotion? She must have been overwhelmed all at once with great conviction over her own sin and the great kindness of Christ, who did not condemn her or drive her away.

The Pharisee, Simon, implied that Jesus did not recognize the depth of this woman's depravity. Simon said to himself, "If this man were a prophet, he would know who is touching him and *what kind* of woman she is—that she is a sinner" (Luke 7:39, emphasis mine). The English words *what kind* in this verse are derived from two Greek words, *poios,* meaning "what," and *dapedon,* meaning "soil." In other words, Simon suggested that Jesus did not clearly comprehend that the "soil" of her life was made up of nothing but compost, dung, sinful muck, and shame-ridden manure. Her "soil" was clearly appalling to the Pharisee, but to the Savior, who takes the dead places of our lives and creates breathtaking beauty, her soil was just right.

> When we have accepted the worst, we have nothing more to lose. And that automatically means we have everything to gain. Dale Carnegie

She knew the shame of her old self, yet her sinful ways could not keep her from courageously reaching out for the lifegiving forgiveness of Christ. She correctly perceived that in Him she could find life. Jesus never downplayed or minimized the sin in her life. He never does. But in His lavish love, Jesus saw beyond the overt, smelly compost of her life and reached into the heart of a broken and contrite woman. Her soil, laced with compost, proved to be the essential amendment for a life of beauty and love.

Just as the Pharisees were criticizing her in their high-minded manner, Jesus, the ultimate Lifegiver, focused on her great love and her overwhelming need for Him. He explained to Simon the Pharisee *that her love was actually in proportion to the forgiveness that she desperately needed.* She loved much because she had been forgiven much. Jesus planted a seed in that repentant woman's heart, and a lifegiving garden began. Her great need for forgiveness provided the ideal compost for germination. Indeed, life was on the way.

Sister, if you feel you are chief among sinners, take heart! If you feel you need more forgiveness than most, be encouraged. *You actually have the most potential for loving and lifegiving!* The woman who knows her need for Christ's lifegiving touch actually has the most potential to love and give life. That is the mystery of the kingdom of God.

The power of the seed

In a garden, each mature plant is filled with seeds that can reproduce that plant many times over. So it is in the life of a lifegiver. From her own life—especially out of the deepest places of her own need—she finds she now has many seeds to sow.

We see this illustrated by the sunflower. The head of a mature sunflower can have 850 seeds in it. A full three-fourths of these seeds can produce life. Imagine that! This is the principle of lifegiving. Just as one seed was responsible for bringing forth one sunflower, now that one sunflower has the potential to bring forth more than five-hundred new blossoms. We can never predict exactly where the seed will land. So in lifegiving, the lifegiver expects a harvest but doesn't always know if she will see it, but when she does, even she is wonderfully amazed.

So it was with my life. I met "Jenny" in an unusual way. It was 1985, and I was a flight attendant for Northwest Airlines. I had just flown in on a 747 from Japan to Chicago on a long all-nighter. I had been up for almost forty hours straight. To say the least, I was tired and crabby, and all I wanted to do was sleep. I had jumped on another flight right away, hoping to see my fiancé, Butch. I had asked the gate agent for a seat where I would not have to sit by anyone. How is that for a lifegiver? Little did I know I was about to sow a small seed that would bring dramatic change in the life of a young woman—let's call her Jenny—and in my own life.

As I boarded the airplane, I looked in vain for a seat by myself. All I could spot was a row toward the back with an open middle seat and a girl in the window seat. I figured that was the best I could find. Exhausted, I fell into the aisle seat, ready to sleep.

Well, you know how God works—with unexpected timing! Little did I understand that I was about to witness a mysterious yet wonderful miracle of God. I would come to see that the risk of my obedience would be the key to unlock a lifegiving treasure. My choice alone would determine the outcome.

> I am a little pencil in the hand of a writing God who is sending a love letter to the world. Mother Teresa

The flight was about two and a half hours long. I had so looked forward to a nap on this flight, to pull the warm blanket around me and snuggle up close to my pillow. I struggled for what seemed like forever to get that pillow just right. I finally got somewhat comfortable, but I could not sleep. I tried everything, but sleep would not come.

As the flight attendant came by to ask for drink orders, I glanced over at the beautiful young woman sitting next to the window. She caught my eye and painfully and reluctantly smiled. I smiled too, yet wondered why she was alone and why she looked so sad. But I was tired after meeting the needs of an airplane filled with 420 people on my previous flight. I did not want to talk to anyone or even be nice for that matter. (How's that for a lifegiving woman!)

But I felt the Lord tug at my heart to speak to this woman. I fought this for what felt like hours. I told the Lord I was certain she was really not all that sad. He said she was. I told Him I didn't want to give out, that I had nothing to give. He said He understood and gently reminded me that is where He comes in. This conversation with the Lord went on and on, taxing my emotions. But through the struggle I knew what I must do. I knew I must obey, even though it seemed that my lifegiving well was dry.

As I turned to speak to this young woman, I saw her peering out the window as if she wished she could fly away to a dreamy, faraway place. I kept fighting the foe of complacency within my heart. Perhaps she would rather be alone. Perhaps I should not interrupt her. Perhaps it really would not matter.

But I knew better. I knew the Lord desired an opportunity to move on her behalf. I said hello and started with some small talk, but she quickly fell silent. I struggled again. *Did it matter anyway? She did not seem to want to talk, so why was I pushing?*

In those few tenuous moments the Lord gently said to me, "All I desire you to do is *speak hope* for the life I long to give her and remind her of *my great love for her.*"

It seemed so simple. Too simple.

Yet despite my discomfort, I felt compelled to share with this lost young girl the words the Lord had given to me. With great reluctance, I stepped out of my comfortable understanding and shared the Lord's message. I told this fragile young woman I had wanted to sleep and that the Lord had not allowed me to. I told her Jesus wanted me to share that He deeply loved her and desired for her to have true, abundant life. God wanted her to know that He is full of grace and mercy and that He so longs to have a loving relationship with her.

She sat there for a very long time, still and quiet. *What in the world am I doing?* I wondered. *She must think I'm a nut!* Moments went by, then minutes. Still she said nothing.

Finally she looked at me, and, hesitantly, she started to open up. She shared through tear-filled eyes that she was on her way to have an abortion. The relationship she had with the father of her baby was short-lived and quite painful. She went on to tell me that her family would be furious with her "lack of discretion." Fear and shame had plunged her into despair. She saw no way out, no way through, and no way to save the life of this child.

For the next hour I spoke life into Jenny. I showed her the hope that only Christ can give. I pointed to a future for her and her child that was possible only in Christ.

As we landed on the hot black tarmac, I asked her if there was anything I could personally do to help her choose life for her baby and herself. She said she did not see how it could ever work. She still saw no way out but thanked me for my care and time. I gave her my home phone in Chicago and said I would do whatever I could to bring life out of this situation. She walked off the airplane a broken young woman. I never thought I would see her again. I felt that I had failed.

But God knew differently! A small but lifegiving seed was planted in Jenny's life that day. All He desired was a seed. He needed me to look beyond my selfish, personal wants to simply obey His leading.

Four months later I received a surprising phone call from Jenny. She was in Chicago and wanted to meet with me. I was very excited to see her, yet I didn't really know what to expect. As I stood in the restaurant waiting for her to arrive, I peered out the window and saw a woman approaching. Little did I understand then, but this would be a defining moment in my life, a magnificent moment in which I understood that *in hearing the voice of the Father and in obeying His gentle prompting, I had touched eternity.*

Every saint has a past and every sinner a future. <small>Sixteenth-century poet</small>

Time seemed to stop as Jenny stood before me, pregnant with her little child, giving that baby life. I started to cry. I cried for her and her precious child, and I cried for me. I cried that I almost said no to the Lord that day. He had asked me to be the honored vessel of His lifegiving message. Oh, what if I had resisted Him and given way to my own desires? In His great love for me, He desired that I would partake in the sweetness of her restoration and healing. The joy and power of lifegiving seemed overwhelming.

Jenny made an adoption plan for her son with a loving Christian family. Jenny gave her child life, and she gave life to a family longing for a child. After the adoption of her son, I heard less and less frequently from Jenny. She married and became a mother to two little girls. I understood that I had become a part of this good yet deeply painful period in her life.

Time passed. We drifted apart. Our lives moved on. Surprisingly, last Christmas, nearly sixteen years after I met Jenny on the plane, I received this letter from her.

> Dear Tammy,
>
> Haven't heard anything from the adoption agency for a few years now. I used to get pictures every year but my social worker has kids now, and I think she has decided to become a full-time mom . . . or maybe

they just stopped sending pictures. Several times I have thought of dropping a note to the agency to see if there is anything in my file . . . anything waiting for me. I just never seem to get around to doing it. I know in my heart that he's okay and things are the way they were meant to be. Hard to believe he just turned fifteen. At times it seems a lifetime ago. Other times it seems like just yesterday.

I want to thank you again for everything you did for me at that time in my life. When I tell people about you, I tell them God sent an angel. When I met you on the airplane, and the entire time I was pregnant, our friendship seemed so natural and normal. As I look back it seems so unbelievably incredible! The way we met . . . of all the seats for you to sit in. The fact that you lived in Chicago and I ended up at my aunt's home there . . . everything fell into place. I don't think I could have survived that experience without you. . . . You kept me strong. . . . You helped me more than I can ever put into words during the most difficult time in my life. . . . You will always have a special place in my heart. . . .

Love,
Jenny

I call that payday.

I call that lifegiving power that fills up and overflows. I call that passion with purpose. I call that true life! Proverbs says that the one who refreshes others will be refreshed. I was the one longing for refreshment that day on the plane. I was tired and weary, and I felt like I had nothing left to give. But, by the grace of God, I gave to Jenny in spite of my own need. Was it a struggle? Yes! Did I want to pass on the call? Yes!

But sister, I received more refreshment than I could have ever imagined! Heda Bejar said, "The fragrance always remains in the hand that gives the rose." The sweet refreshment we receive when we give to another is one of the most powerful secrets of being a lifegiver. This truth has given me so much encouragement as I continue to daily give my life away.

Jenny's story began with a seed, a small seed of truth that God planted in her life. It seemed like a tiny, insignificant seed, the kind Jesus talks about in Mark 4:31–32: "The kingdom of God is like a mustard seed, the smallest seed you plant in the ground. But when planted, this seed grows and becomes the largest of all garden plants. It produces large branches, and the wild birds can make nests in its shade" (NCV).

When we say yes to lifegiving, it isn't just to grand and lofty deeds. It is often the small deeds or the simple words that grow to have the largest lifegiving impact. Mother Teresa said, "We can do no great things, only small things with great love." The world is crying out for love. I know you wonder if your feeble attempts to plant seeds will ever last and make a tangible difference. But friend, remember, true greatness always starts with the least likely, the most needy, and the smallest seed.

Time to grow

The lifegiver has confidence that God will cause the seed to bring forth life. Her expectation is placed in Him. In Mark 4:26–29, Jesus said, "This is what the kingdom of God is like. A man scatters seed on the ground. Night and day, whether he sleeps or gets up, the seed sprouts and grows, though he does not know how. All by itself the soil produces grain—first the stalk, then the head, then the full kernel in the head. As soon as the grain is ripe, he puts the sickle to it, because the harvest has come." The lifegiving woman plants the seed and, like the sower in the parable, how it grows, she does not know. But she doesn't go digging it up, either!

There are times when we start to see growth, but it seems slow. The Bible says, "Do not despise these small beginnings" (Zechariah 4:10 NLT). When we first step out into a lifestyle of lifegiving, our seed offerings seem especially feeble. You may decide to finally show some hospitality to a new family in the church, only to burn dinner or have your children run naked through the house! (Oh yes, it happened to me!) Do not despise small beginnings! Rather, laugh about it, go get some carryout, and dress (and threaten!) that child again. You gain momentum and confidence by attempting a lifegiving lifestyle over and over, again and again. You will grow in grace, confidence, and humor over time. Do not despise the first season of growth for anything in your life. Even this message of lifegiving has been a process in my life.

> Happiness is like a cat. If you try to coax it or call it, it will avoid you; it will never come. But if you pay no attention to it and go about your business, you'll find it rubbing against your leg and jumping into your lap! William Bennett

Sisters, nothing is wasted in Christ! All of our tears, all of our pain, all forgiven sin can turn into life-producing power in our lives and through our lives! Nothing is wasted. As Psalm 126:5 reminds us, "Those who sow in tears will reap with songs of joy."

A small beginning, a powerful God

Jenny's story and stories like hers are being lived out daily in the lives of quiet lifegivers. Their small, simple offerings are woven into the tapestry of a lifestyle of lifegiving. These are not just their stories; these are your stories too. Opportunities are all around you.

The moment you take a risk and present yourself as an offering to the Lord is the instant you begin to plant your seeds. In time, you will find that you have planted a garden of beauty and might. That, my friend, is the magnificent design of the Lord's lifegiving plan.

Friend, can you see yourself here? Have you looked past the small and simple things, thinking that God can only use the seemingly grand and impressive things?

Helen Keller said, "I long to accomplish a great and noble task, but it is my chief duty to accomplish small tasks as if they were great and noble." You see, even small tasks of lifegiving become seed-bearing, life-changing events in the hand of God. With only one small seed, a life can forever be transformed. When we provide the seed, He brings forth dramatic change both in the lives of others and most surprisingly in our own. (See 1 Corinthians 3:5–10.)

"Unless a grain of wheat falls into the ground and dies . . . "

Not only does the lifegiving woman plant good seeds into the lives of others, but her very life is also a seed that is to be planted. Jesus actually foretold His death when He said, "Unless a grain of wheat falls into the ground and dies, it remains alone; but if it dies, it produces much grain" (John 12:24 NKJV). Through Christ's willingness to allow His human body, His natural life, to die, He was able to rise again and give us the hope of eternal life.

The message of Christ is clear: we are to imitate Him in His death (Philippians 3:10). As Dietrich Bonhoeffer said, "Jesus bids us come and die."[3] There is something so freeing and glorious about releasing our self-centered lives in order to find Christ's abundant life. "He himself bore our sins in his body on the tree, so that we might die to sins and live for righteousness; by his wounds you have been healed" (1 Peter 2:24).

> We cannot make something where nothing existed—whether it be a poem, a house, or a painting—without breathing life into it so that it may itself breathe. Elizabeth O'Connor

At times, all of us feel that we have nothing to give. Did you know that this is a good thing? It is actually when we feel we can do nothing of great value in our own strength that Christ can finally do something through us! It is in our weakness that He is glorified (2 Corinthians 12:8–11). It is in our dying that we live. It is in losing our own sinful, willful lives that we find real life. It is the work of the Word of God that puts to death our old natural life that is often wrought with self-will, that is easily hurt and disappointed, that expects something in return when it gives. It is when this natural life dies that we can begin to walk in the power of the resurrected life of Christ. This is the mystery of giving our lives away.

The outer shell of the self-life

We long to live this way, but we often feel trapped and unable to start. The outer shell of our self-life may keep us from giving life to others. Look again at what happens to the seed when it falls into the ground to die. In the dark, moist earth, the outer shell of the seed begins to soften and crack open. It is only when this outer shell cracks open that the lifegiving potential of the seed is released. You see, all the life inside that little seed is held captive within that hard outer shell.

The outer shell is so strong that it literally has the lifegiving potential of that little seed locked down. Did you know that seeds have been found in pyramids that are thousands of years old? When those seeds were planted—placed in the proper soil with the proper nutrients—they grew into plants. It merely took the right conditions to break through and set free the life of that seed!

This is just how we are. God has fashioned us as lifegivers. We carry within us the powerful potential of the seed. Yet we all have outer shells with which we must contend. These powerful outer shells can keep us from being the lifegiving women we long to be.

What is the outer shell anyway? Sister, it is often so subtle. It may not look evil or seem like obvious sin. This outer shell, the self-life, keeps us from being true lifegivers. Yes, the self-life can look good, but it brings a deadly blow. It includes self-righteousness, self-confidence, self-satisfaction, and self-will.

Don't say things. What you are stands over you the while, and thunders so that I cannot hear what you say to the contrary.

Ralph Waldo Emerson

Self-righteousness

Perhaps personal sins of self-righteousness have never crossed your mind, yet I think this one is the easiest to identify. The self-righteous, hard road of the do-gooder is in sharp contrast to the peaceful (well, okay, messy and a little crazy at times!) path of the lifegiver. The big difference is that the lifegiver is God-focused, and the do-gooder is self-focused.

Have you ever been met by a good deed that had a hidden sting? It's the one that leaves you feeling like you owe something, or it's the favor done with the unspoken implication, "I slaved all day for you, and now I expect something in return." I think we are all guilty of this from time to time. In contrast, the lifegiver gives without expecting anything in return, no reciprocation or even praise. She continues to serve, knowing that her true reward is with her heavenly Father. (More on that later!)

Self-confidence

Perhaps your biggest struggle is self-confidence. You may feel intimidated by the thought of having someone over for a snappy appetizer or two. But there is a big difference between God-confidence and self-confidence. It is not that we shouldn't have confidence to move successfully in a task set before us. Rather, we should understand and deeply trust in the power of the living God. It is He who gives and creates lifegiving confidence.

This looks much different than simple self-confidence, and sister, this is a good thing. Having confidence in God alone frees us from the pressure to control every situation and encourages us to take risks. Jeremiah 17:7–8 emphasizes the great harvest we can have when we act with God-confidence: "But blessed are those who trust in the Lord and have made the Lord their hope and confidence. They are like trees planted along a riverbank, with roots that reach deep into the water. Such trees are not bothered by the heat or worried by long months of drought. Their leaves stay green, and they go right on producing delicious fruit" (NLT). It is never anything *in us* that accounts for the Lord's blessings *to us*. Everything we are given is from Him.

Self-satisfaction

Or, dear friend, maybe you have struggled with the self-life of self-satisfaction. For some of us, self-satisfaction means we go to endless extremes to avoid change, to reject correction, and to keep things status quo. We fear that someone may demand more of us than we are comfortable giving out. Personal comfort is key. Situations where uneasiness is immanent are avoided at all costs.

It is not a matter of our equipment, but a matter of our poverty; not of what we bring with us, but of what God puts into us. Oswald Chambers

Yet self-satisfaction is the enemy to a life of growth and beauty. This very thick and selfish outer shell must be broken so that true abundant life can come forth. Things like self-sufficiency, selfishness, arrogance, and prideful thoughts—*I am better than this; I don't deserve this; don't they know who I am?*—all these must go the way of the cross. *You and I are meant to follow in the steps of our Lord, not avoid them.* Every opportunity we have to die to self-satisfaction is an opportunity to know the joy of the Lord, which comes by way of the cross.

Self-will
Of all the self-life components, perhaps none is as powerful or damaging as self-will. This rigid shell demands attention, lives for self-glory, rears its ugly head, keeps count of lengthy offenses, and knows no other path than hostility to the will of God. It is the antithesis of all lifegiving.

Yet Christ Himself cried out to the Father, "Yet not my will, but yours be done" (Luke 22:42). This, my friend, is the lifegiver's prayer. Clearly, the most effective way to crack open the outer shell of self-will is to welcome the work of the Holy Spirit over and over again. In fact, we must learn to see in every difficult situation an opportunity to die to the self-life.

Recently I was involved in a very difficult conversation. I felt terribly misunderstood, misjudged, and emotionally manipulated. Many self-willed, self-justifying thoughts flooded my mind. I was deeply hurt and angry. Yet, as I was driving home that evening, the Lord spoke to me these difficult yet freeing words: "See in this a chance to die." See in all things, in everything, a chance to die to self and the pride that comes from defending yourself and your rights.

Do you feel a bit discouraged right now? Are you overwhelmed by the ugly side of your self-life? Take heart, dear friend; this is the hard road to the cross that must be walked by every true lifegiver. She who understands her self-life must fall from its pedestal. There is only one reigning King, and it is Christ Himself! He is her ultimate Lifegiver and the supreme role model for a selfless lifestyle.

Though not without struggle, the woman who wants to walk as a redeemed lifegiver walks the road to the cross and gives her all that others may receive life. She is peaceful, calm, and generous in spirit because she has another source for her reward. She doesn't look to those to whom she gives for accolades. She takes no notice of the lack of praise *or* the cheers, for she has done her work, she has served, she has sweat, she has walked, she has touched each one as unto the Lord. The outer shell of self-life has been broken, and the power of His life is being revealed through her.

All seeds contain life

Never forget the power of life in a seed. A plant's entire potential is contained in a tiny seed. To plant seeds and expect a good harvest, we realize that all life experiences—the good, the bad, and the worst— work together in God's plan to create soil for seed.

The seeds we plant in others' lives promise the harvest. As Jenny's life illustrates, we never know how much a little seed may grow. But the hope of the harvest keeps us planting!

Each of our own lives is also like a seed. The outer shell of the seed that must break open is our self-life. Those of us who love Jesus are willing to be broken open. We say yes to this temporary pain, knowing that—as in the death and resurrection of Christ—this process alone allows real life to come forth.

chapter four

The Good Gardener

gardener

Lord, purge our eyes to see within

the seed a tree

Within the glowing egg a bird,

Within the shroud a butterfly.

Till, taught by such we see beyond

all creatures . . . Thee . . .

Christina Rossetti

Lifegiving is not a treasure to be hidden; it is a gift to be shared. The lifestyle of lifegiving is like a beautiful garden, cultivated carefully by the Master Gardener. It is a blessing that is meant to be shared with those around us. When we tend our lives like a beautiful garden, our lifestyle becomes alluring to the world. The underlying value, the true attraction to those around us, is our reflection of Christ Himself.

Whom do you touch daily? Neighbors, teachers, coworkers, children, husband, parents? If you are a young mother, your natural place to give life is to your children and other young mothers, perhaps in a play group or through a preschool. If you are a grandmother or an older woman, you have a special ministry, described in Titus 2:3–4: "Teach the older women to live in a way that is appropriate for someone serving the Lord. . . . These older women must train the younger women to love their husbands and their children" (NLT). The principle that Titus is emphasizing here is mentorship. A forty-year-old woman or even a twenty-year-old is an older woman to someone! We have the opportunity to sow lifegiving seed in our unique sphere of influence in every different season of our lives.

The Bible also teaches that when we give unto the Lord in a sacrificial way, when we are faithful to the area He has called us to, *He will indeed enlarge our lifegiving potential!* We will not be able to contain the goodness of the Lord. "Enlarge the place of your tent, stretch your tent curtains wide, do not hold back; lengthen your cords, strengthen your stakes. For you will spread out to the right and to the left" (Isaiah 54:2–3). When we are faithful to share life with those around us, God will continue to expand our territory, increase our store of seed, and enlarge the harvest.

God requires much of those to whom He has entrusted much (Luke 12:48). This principle applies during every season of our lives. If you have more time in your life, then this becomes your area of good soil and accountability. This is your seedbed of sorts. If you have financial resources, cultivate your area with living a generous lifestyle, giving as you would to the Lord Jesus Himself. If you have an extra bedroom in your home, share with the poor wanderer, or if you enjoy cooking, share your food with the hungry.

Growth is the only evidence of life. John Henry Newman

Annual and perennial lifegiving

A lifegiver also realizes that some of her planting is of the annual variety and some the perennial. Some people come into our lives for a season. We give of ourselves and plant seeds that bring dramatic change in their lives for a time. But then our lives move apart in different directions. This is God's design. Other lifegiving is perennial and tends to multiply within our own sphere. Perennial plants come back in greater number and fullness each year. Eventually we may divide these wonderful plants and pass them along to one or five or even ten friends. Soon the beauty and fragrance of the garden has been transplanted into many other gardens across town. We are meant to share our long-term family relationships and friendships with others. These relationships will continue to grow deep and return year after year in greater splendor and glory.

Because it is sure of its beauty, the rose makes terrible demands on us. Alain Meillard, 20th-century American rose breeder

---

Seasons of renewal

All good farmers know that rotating their crops is essential for the soil to continue to bring life. If the same crop selection is planted with each passing season, the soil will become void of certain nutrients and no longer give life. This principle also holds true in the lifegiver's garden. Allowing God to move you from a place where you feel secure to a place that will produce additional life is a key ingredient for a lifestyle of lifegiving. For most of us, that is very difficult to do. We tightly cling to the familiar places that feel secure. Just when we get comfortable tending our little lifegiving garden, God says, "Time to rotate! Time to do something new! Give to new people."

In all things of nature there is something of the marvelous. Aristotle

The thought of a move, a financial adjustment, a new child, or a different status in life may make us want to curl up and die. We go to great lengths to protect our comfortable gardens. But the Lord is always doing a new and purposeful thing. As the ultimate Creator, He finds joy in seeing us become the vessels of beauty and purpose He designed us to be. And sometimes that means rotating the crops.

A good gardener also uses pruning sheers to cut back growth, with the ultimate goal of producing even more life. A gardener knows that for a plant that is thriving to continue to produce life, pruning must occur. Timely pruning repairs damage before further problems can occur. It also encourages greater quantity and quality of fruit and flowers. Pruning can shape a plant so that it is more attractive and better able to withstand heavy snow and storms. It stimulates and directs growth.

So it is with the lifegiving woman. Not only does she allow the pruning process to occur, but she welcomes it, fully understanding it is this very process that will bring forth a beautiful life. She understands that to direct new growth, to increase her fruit and flowers, to keep damage and disease at bay, to become strong in the face of snow and storms, she must trust that the Master Gardener knows what He is doing. His timing is always perfect. He is pruning with a purpose. *God does not want us to stay stagnant in our successes or failures.* He is determined and passionate to be doing new things in our lifegiving journey.

Go out on a limb . . . that's where the fruit is. Mark Twain

Even what is pruned is not lost. The pruned parts become an integral part of future lifegiving as they are chopped up and tilled back into the soil. As a matter of fact, for the gardener or farmer, the more years this process goes on, the richer and more fertile the land becomes. The lifegiver who starts by planting small seeds, who plants a harvest of life in others and submits to the process of pruning can count on a rich garden of lifegiving.

chapter five

The Secret Place

secret place

Those things are

dearest to us that

cost us most.

Michel de Montaigne

All the motivation of the lifegiving woman issues forth from one central place: *the secret place of her life hidden in Christ.* All of us live two lives: what we allow the world to see and what is really happening within our hearts. The external stuff we spend our lives grooming so that we appear beautiful, in control, and put together. Yet it is the inward person, the transparent heart, that truly concerns God. He longs for our outward appearance to match our inward reality. So before we travel to the outward expression of the lifegiving lifestyle, we first must burrow deeper into the secret place of the lifegiver. *Here we see revealed the mystery of her true power.* Here her heart is exposed for what it truly is.

The inner sanctuary of the lifegiver's heart is holy ground. This is where God dwells. Her inner life is the headquarters of the lifegiving lifestyle, the power plant, command central, where God is enthroned. This secret place is by definition a hidden, unseen place. It is unseen by people but seen very clearly by God. Here, God alone sees the lifegiver's sacrificial and powerful love. This intimate, private place is where the lifegiving woman finds true life-changing beauty and depth. It is the secret place, the secret sanctuary.

The three acts of righteousness
Secret service
When we look at the great strength that flows out of the lifegiving woman's lifestyle, we see it finds its roots in Matthew 6:1–4. Jesus reveals this secret, yet most powerful, place:

> Be careful not to do your "acts of righteousness" before men, to be seen by them. If you do, you will have no reward from your Father in heaven.
> So when you give to the needy, do not announce it

with trumpets, as the hypocrites do in the synagogues and on the streets, to be honored by men. I
tell you the truth, they have received their reward in
full. But when you give to the needy, do not let your
left hand know what your right hand is doing, so that
your giving may be in secret. Then your Father, who
sees what is done in secret, will reward you.

The lifegiving woman does her loving acts of service for His eyes
only. This is such a beautiful gift to God. Scripture clearly tells us that
these acts of secret service will be rewarded.

Essentially, God has set up an eternal bank account for each of
us. Jesus encouraged us to lay up treasures in heaven (Matthew
6:19–21). This is not an attempt to earn our acceptance from God—
He has already accepted us through Christ. Rather, this laying up of
treasures allows us to pursue God's pleasure. Every act of service,
each lifegiving activity, is like a deposit into this heavenly account.
Even the simple and mundane acts of daily giving and loving that are
unseen by others are conducted in the full sight of our unseen God.
And God, who sees in secret, will be pleased with us and will reward
us openly. Like the heart of a child who trusts his mother to keep his
prized possessions, so the lifegiving woman trusts God to keep
record of her deeds done in secret.

It gives me a deep, comforting sense that things seen are temporal
and things unseen are eternal. Helen Keller

Last spring, my friend Maryjo visited us here in beautiful
Colorado. We took the children on a walk in the mountains. As we
were walking, her four-year-old son Eli came running up to us. "Mom,
look at the tiger rock I found!" Maryjo studied it very carefully and

gushed about what a great treasure it was. After a few moments of careful concentration, Eli said, "Mom, will you put the rock in your pocket until we get home? It will be safe there." Eli did not even trust himself to keep track of his most treasured possession! He knew that only his trusted mom could keep it safe. With the same childlike trust, the lifegiving woman believes that her God will keep her deeds in His pocket. He treasures the things she does in secret. She has learned to put her confidence in God, the One who will keep her secrets safe and will lovingly reward her.

> Many things I have tried to grasp, and have lost. That which I have placed in God's hands I still have. Martin Luther

Closet treasures

The second secret act of righteousness that Jesus describes in Matthew 6:5–6 is prayer. "And when you pray, do not be like the hypocrites, for they love to pray standing in the synagogues and on the street corners to be seen by men. I tell you the truth, they have received their reward in full. But when you pray, go into your room, close the door and pray to your Father, who is unseen. Then your Father, who sees what is done in secret, will reward you."

Certainly, prayer is the foundation of her life. And Jesus specifies that it is *secret* prayer. She speaks and listens to the unseen God behind the closed door of her closet. She understands that this time alone, quiet before God, provides the power and strength to live out the lifegiving lifestyle. This conversation is intimate, dynamic, and safe. She postures herself in this secret place to find a deeper understanding of the ways of the Father and to commune with her closest of all friends. It is not for exhibition; it is for intimacy. And it is her loving Friend who hears in secret who will reward her openly.

A LIFESTYLE OF FORGIVENESS

Jesus teaches many things about how to pray in this passage. One important idea I would highlight is the importance of forgiving others. Forgiveness in secret is very important to God. "If you forgive those who sin against you, your heavenly Father will forgive you" (Matthew 6:14 NLT).

Lifegiving women must live *a lifestyle of forgiveness*. We must forgive our children because they do not understand the sacrifices we make for them, forgive women who cannot return kindness to us when we have reached out to them, forgive our husbands when they do not meet up to our expectations, forgive our parents when they have wounded us, forgive our bosses when they pass over us for a promotion. On and on the list of forgiveness goes. Lifegiving women understand that they are sinners in need of forgiveness, so they are able to forgive others who have wounded and disappointed them.

The lifegiving woman knows that she must forgive to be forgiven. While forgiving others their reckless sins, she is crying out with Christ, "Father, forgive them, for they do not know what they are doing" (Luke 23:34). Then she is able to keep loving, to keep giving, to keep serving in His strength. Forgiveness is a choice whereby the life-giver allows Jesus to take away everything that would potentially rob her of her secret reward. By forgiving those who do not notice, do not appreciate, do not give back, she is obeying her Lord's command. She maintains her humble position, knowing that she has been forgiven and that she can and must forgive others.

Often, the sins of others against us are reckless; they are not premeditated or motivated out of evil intent. They are thoughtless oversights or immature responses to our love. But these verses also mention the willful sins of others, the evil done intentionally.

Many years ago, I found myself involved in an abusive and quite hurtful relationship. The shame and pain were at times overwhelming. I felt I deserved to bask in my unforgiveness. *How could I just let this person off the hook, release this person? What if it happens again?* I became imprisoned by the negative choices I had made. I was a prisoner to more than the hurtful deeds done against me; my soul was confined in a horrendous prison of anger and resentment that I had built with my own hands, offense by offense.

Charity, to be fruitful, must cost us. Mother Teresa

Through intimate prayer and the gentle work of the Holy Spirit, I began to see that it was Christ's death and His forgiveness of my gruesome sin that held the keys to my freedom. Like the sinful woman in Luke 7, I became deeply aware of the wickedness of my heart and my deep need for forgiveness. As the Holy Spirit revealed my great imprisonment, I was free to see forgiveness the way Christ does. None of us deserve mercy and life; we all deserve judgment and death. Yet, because of His great love for us, we can receive true life and freedom from the effects of devastating sin.

Friend, though the truth often carries a sting, it is the only power that will free you. Engage in a fair wrestling match with truth. Examine your heart to see if you have areas of unforgiveness imprisoning you. Have you felt the pain of sin done against you but have not known how to free yourself from the bitterness and resentment? Yes, this is difficult. But when you bring these self-imposed sentences to the secret place of prayer, ask Christ to forgive the sin of bitterness in your heart and release those who have hurt you. A beautiful miracle will unfold. The unseen Father who sees what is done in secret will reward your obedience. He will exchange your heart of stone for a heart of flesh. Remember, we are not just saved from sin and death (as if that were not enough), but we have been saved for abundant life! Jesus, your faithful Friend, will give you grace to live the abundant life you never thought possible. That's why they call it the Good News . . . because it really is.

Fasting for life

Jesus concludes His description of the three acts of righteousness with instructions on fasting. "When you fast, do not look somber as the hypocrites do, for they disfigure their faces to show men they are fasting. I tell you the truth, they have received their reward in full. But when you fast, put oil on your head and wash your face, so that it will not be obvious to men that you are fasting, but only to your Father, who is unseen; and your Father, who sees what is done in secret, will reward you" (Matthew 6:16–18).

What is fasting, anyway? Most of us would say that fasting is going without food to show God that we are serious about something. I agree. But I think it is much more than that.

It's a very big idea to God.

Come with me down a road that is full of opportunity, risk, and change. While we develop the big picture of what fasting is, you must understand what you are up against. Your ideas of fasting *food* will pale in comparison to the fasting of your *life*. The Enemy, Satan, longs to see you live a life of comfort and safety. But this is where Jesus challenges us to press into faith.

Think with me about the broader concept of fasting. You may need to "fast" a dream or a desire during a given season of your life. Immediately you might be wondering how you can fast something you love for a season of your life. Let me explain. First, this fast will look different for each of us. Perhaps you must fast a dream you long to see fulfilled, a loving marriage relationship, the privilege of becoming a parent, or a ministry you have always desired to have. No matter what the fast may be, *it is always connected to what we secretly desire and deeply love.* Though these desires may be godly and pure, if they are fulfilled before we are ready, then they have the potential to destroy us. Fasting food may be difficult for our weak flesh. Foregoing a heartfelt dream is much more difficult.

THE FAST OF MY LIFE

It was 1991, and I had just ended my ten-year career as a flight attendant to stay home with our ever-growing family. As a stay-at-home mom, I was already fasting my career goals. Little did I know that a "three-day fast" was soon to become a "forty-day fast."

Mackenzie was three years old, and we had just adopted our four-month-old son, Samuel, from Korea. We had recently moved from Virginia Beach, where Butch worked for Pat Robertson, back to Dallas. Our time in Virginia close to family was wonderful. I had always lived away from my family, and the benefit of having a grandmother and extended family close by was such a help. Yet God in His infinite wisdom had a different plan. It was, in fact, a fasting plan. We packed up and moved back to Dallas.

It was the beginning of what I call my Ninevah experience. Dallas prepares anyone to hate hell. There are the miserable, boiling hot, lava-like months of summer—not to mention all those large cockroaches! It really makes you desire assurance of your salvation! (If you're from Texas, relax. I lived there another nine years and sobbed when I left.) I must admit that I did not want to move. I went kicking and screaming all the way. I knew God's hand was in it. I was just hoping it was not going to be another death to another dream.

When we arrived in Dallas, life was infused with busyness. I had a whole house to make into a home. During those first days, I carried

Sam draped around my neck, and Mackenzie was usually at my feet having a tea party. All I could manage to do was unpack one box per hour. Talk about discouraging! I had no close friends or extended family nearby, and we had not connected with a church yet. And I had no airline job to retreat to. I think it was weeks before I took my first shower.

These first months in Dallas were full of paralyzing loneliness and isolation. My husband, Butch, was traveling about 250 days a year, working hard to provide for our now one-income family. I understood why he was gone; I just hated that he was. I thought life was already full of deprivations. Little did I know I was about to embrace the most difficult fast of my life.

Love has an amazing law of return. If we have love, it will come back to us by some means or path. We don't get to choose how it will come back, but there will always be compensation far greater than what we've been given. And it may only be in eternity that we will reap its full consequences. Stormie Omartian

---

As our first year in Texas passed, I made a few friends, and we got plugged in to a good church. I was starting to take comfort in the notion that soon I would have control of my life back. After all, I had stayed at home with my children *full-time* for almost two years! Before long, it would be *my* time again, and quite honestly, I couldn't wait.

That was just about the time Butch came home from a two-week trip to Russia. He had filmed a music video for the Christian group 4HIM, which supported the American Bible Society. They had been listening and responding to the profound stories of the former underground church. The passion the Russian people had for Christ was convicting.

While Butch was in Russia, he visited a few orphanages to see firsthand the plight of the orphaned children. It was reported that there were over 450,000 children living in orphanages in Moscow. Adoption was an unfamiliar concept to them. There was no legal standard for domestic adoption, let alone international adoption. Butch was deeply troubled for these children who needed a family.

As I was helping Butch unpack from his trip, I listened to story after story of the way God was working in big ways in Russia. I loved sharing his experiences with him. But without warning the tables turned. Butch suddenly started trespassing on my carefully laid plans.

The soul though it is hidden is at all times revealed, expressing itself through everything we say and do. Through the ordinary brush strokes of our everyday life, a portrait of our souls is being painted.

Ken Gire

"Tammy, I really think we need to think about adopting an older child from Russia. I am deeply burdened by the hopelessness of the children I saw there, the pain in their eyes, their broken and desperate spirits." On and on he spoke. All I could see was an endless life of macaroni and cheese and bologna sandwiches!

Then came the clincher: "Tammy, I have prayed about this, and I believe there is a child that ... (pause) ... is ours ... (long pause) ... she is waiting for her family."

Looking at my shocked face, he must have felt compelled to add, "Please just pray about it." Now those are fighting words. Just pray about it? What's that supposed to mean? Yes, I would pray—that God would find the right family for this little child. The *right* family, just not *my* family.

I was so angry with Butch that I was determined to make it clear how absurd this idea was for our family and for me. I huffed and *ecret place*

puffed loudly, daily. Finally, I had just been getting my feet and ego back under me. Another child would only mean more work, more sacrifice, more than what I wanted to give. I felt justified in my case. After all, *I* would be the one to deal with the enormous needs of this child while *he* traveled on business most of the year.

Now don't get me wrong. I love kids. I loved adopting kids. I just didn't want any more of either.

So I decided to do what any other woman would do. I called a friend. I wanted to talk to a faithful friend who would come to my worthy defense. Yes, I knew the perfect one. As soon as she answered the phone, I began my self-validation. "You are simply not going to believe this. Sit down. Ready? Well . . . (big sigh) . . . Butch thinks we should adopt another child. Right now! (bigger sigh) . . . We already have a one- and three-year-old. . . . What *is* that man thinking? . . . Well, he is *never* here. I mean, really, an older child? It's not like he's the one who will be putting his life on hold for the next ten years. . . . I am at my limit, and he wants a child with serious medical problems . . . not only that but he is asking me to *pray about it!* Well, don't get me wrong. It's not that I don't want her to have a family. Really I do. Well, of course I do. But let's be honest here. Is it so bad for me to want . . . well, *my* dreams, *my* time, *my* life? I just can't do this. . . . I just can't. . . . No, it will put me six feet under."

To this, my dear friend said, "Oh, Tammy, listen. I really think you *can* do this with the Lord's strength. I believe He has called you to great things, and I believe this child is to be yours . . . blah . . . blah . . . blah . . . "

I did what any other woman would do. I called another friend. I was sure this friend would take my side. I pumped up the challenge a bit. She seemed to be listening, so I went on and on and on. Finally after about fifteen minutes of why it could never work and how he had no idea what he was asking of me, she paused and quietly replied, "Tammy, you're right. You will live a life of dying to yourself, dying to how you think God works. You will need to fast your dreams and desires for a season, and yes, this could be the hardest thing you've ever embraced. It may push you to the edge, demand everything of you, make you wonder if it just isn't much too big for you. But that's okay, because that's where God comes in, and He comes in big."

She nailed it. And I knew it. I just sat there, numb, a bit sick to my stomach.

Character is what you are in the dark. Dwight L. Moody

My good friend Lisa Bevere says, "What you justify, you buy." It wasn't like I was all that selfish. I had adopted one child. There are not many people who have done that! (Here it comes—justify, justify, justify.) And I was a fairly good mother, dedicated and loving. I did put my career on hold for the betterment of my children. (More of that nauseating justification stuff.) So I kept asking my pious self, *Why should I enter a territory that may mean really, really giving my life away? God, don't You want me to be happy? Of course You do, right?* Although I tried hard to justify my position, God stood firmly by His.

So I replied to the Lord, "Okay, Lord, You know I feel overwhelmed, overwrought, overdone. I have no family here. Butch is traveling almost 250 days a year, and God, You know I am not the stay-at-home type (whatever that means!). Really, God, most people just have two kids, two healthy kids. Why should I feel guilty about not wanting more? What about my feelings, God? How, how, how will *I* do this?"

Yes, that was the problem from the start. It was all about the "I" in my life.

That night I sat, broken, at my small kitchen table. I cried out to God for a lifegiving touch. I pleaded with my Savior to heed my case. He brought me to Isaiah 58. Here was an intense dialogue between seemingly righteous people and the living, holy God. These so-called lovers of God had been fasting and praying, yet they saw no supernatural move on God's part. In this convicting passage, God blasts their false humility and goes on to say the following:

> Let us believe that God is in all our simple deeds, and learn to find Him there. A. W. Tozer

Is not this the kind of fasting I have chosen:
to loose the chains of injustice
    and untie the cords of the yoke,
to set the oppressed free
    and break every yoke?
Is it not to share your food with the hungry
    and to provide the poor wanderer with shelter—
when you see the naked, to clothe him?
(Isaiah 58:6–7)

I knew God was speaking directly to me. "But Lord," I said. "What if I can't do it? What if I will never be happy again, what if I fall apart, or worse yet, break apart? What if I fail?"

The Holy Spirit said, "It is all about if/then choices, Tammy. *If* you obey Me, *then* you are granted the promise. *If* you choose a lifestyle of godly fasting, *then* you will get God's attention and His lifegiving promises."

I kept reading.

Then your light will break forth like the dawn,
    and your healing will quickly appear;

> then your righteousness will go before you,
>   and the glory of the LORD will be your rear guard.
> Then you will call, and the LORD will answer;
>   you will cry for help, and he will say: Here am I. . . .
> if you spend yourselves in behalf of the hungry
>   and satisfy the needs of the oppressed,
> then your light will rise in the darkness,
>   and your night will become like the noonday.
> The Lord will guide you always;
>   he will satisfy your needs in a sun-scorched land
>   and will strengthen your frame.
> You will be like a well-watered garden,
>   like a spring whose waters never fail. . . .
> you will be called Repairer of Broken Walls,
>   Restorer of Streets with Dwellings. . . .
> I will cause you to ride on the heights of the land.
> (Isaiah 58:8–14)

I knew in that moment that God was asking me to release my life of safety into His skillful yet fiery hands. My Savior was longing for me to risk and ride on the heights of the land.

That night I said yes to God. *Yes* to a new way of walking and a new dance in a new land. I said yes to soaring within grace I had never known before. My Jesus was calling me to give my life away, and though I was fearful, I knew that He could be trusted because He was good. The power to deny ourselves what we most long for comes from trusting a *good* God whom we love more than anything else on earth.

Safety is what I longed for. But safety never costs us anything. Safety requires no faith. God is not, has never been, and will never be *safe,* in the sense of predictable, easy comfort. But oh, He is good! "You are good, and what you do is good" (Psalm 119:68).

When we learn to trust the goodness of our God, we can then release control of our lives and the areas that hold us in paralyzing fear. No, God is not safe. The Bible says He is a consuming fire. He is not like the safe gods we long to control, safe gods that are powerless to forgive us, shake us, and stir us. These complacent gods slumber and sleep while we pace to and fro, longing for a god with a watchful eye, an arm sure to save. We both love and loathe them. Secretly, we know they demand nothing, and they will deliver nothing. It is only when we understand that the true and living God is something to be reckoned with that we will be launched into a life full of risk and great reward.

When I give, I give myself. Walt Whitman

We started all the paperwork necessary to bring Tatiana home from Russia. Three months into this fast, I discovered I was pregnant with a very *unplanned* child. How could this be happening to me? Another child! (As if God Himself were ever surprised.) I had been concerned about having three children under five, and soon I would be a mother of *four* children under five!

This added stress nearly put me under. I became very sick the first trimester of my pregnancy and looked like a concentration camp survivor—twenty weeks along weighing only ninety-eight pounds. I was always tired and clearly remember telling Butch that I had reached an all-time low—lusting after *sleep!* (I am sure that when mothers die and go to heaven, we get to sleep for the first three months. No interruptions, and no questions asked!)

Every day I struggled with doubt. How would I manage Butch's travel? How would I have energy to parent four small children? How would we pay for another adoption and another baby? I battled moment by moment to understand God's ways. Fighting, planning, warring.

No, God is not safe, and He has not called us to live safe lives. He has called us into a wild, passion-filled rumba, and yes, it is the dance of freedom. Faith is, after all, a dance of the heart. It dances with God in the dark, as it does in the day. Many days it was very dark. Oh, but the music played on. All I can tell you is that God was great at being God that year.

Love is love's reward. John Dryden

Mikia was born on a hot Texas August evening. When she was two weeks old and Samuel was two and Mackenzie was four, Butch left for a month-long trip to Russia to bring Tatiana home to this forever family. Yes, it was a difficult year. Being a mother to a five-year-old child who spoke no English, who had never lived with a family, who ate only ten different foods (none of which we had), who saw kissing, hugging, and attachment as an unwelcome enemy, was difficult at best. There were many nights when I cried out to God to speak into my loneliness, to touch me with a supernatural, lifegiving touch, to dull the isolation I often felt. There were days when Tatiana's food-hiding would catch up with me, her outbursts of screaming and terror would drain every lifegiving reserve I could muster, and her deep neediness would engulf me. I never doubted God's presence, but I so longed to hear His reassuring voice, see His compassionate face, and feel His warm hand upon my weary shoulder. Some days this seemed tangible; some days it didn't. Still the music played on.

Did we all cry at the overwhelming frustration at times? Oh yes. Did I wonder if the potential for healing was possible, if the whirlwind of neediness would destroy our young marriage, if this little girl would ever feel like a part of our family? Yes, yes, oh yes.

But I learned that in this place of lifegiving fasting lay a treasure that no one could steal, no moth or rust could destroy. This was a period in which I knew I was either being broken or made, destroyed or rebuilt, crushed or redeemed. And oh, how we grew. We saw the hand of the living God in big and powerful ways. It is His style after all—big and powerful, unassuming and gentle, always good.

I can tell you it was a year I truly met the Savior, my gentle Healer, my strong Deliverer. I was desperate for Him and for His great love. My Shepherd guided me and satisfied all my needs in a sun-scorched land, and yes, He strengthened my weary frame. He was faithful. I will never, ever be the same.

So how about you, dear friend? Is it time you came boldly before God? Has your great High Priest been speaking to you? Perhaps you bypassed a fast, afraid you would never have food to nourish your soul again. Perhaps you are longing for safety, yet you realize that safety will never save you, shake you, or free you. Yes, you know it will never satisfy the longing of your soul.

Sister, I encourage you today to take God at His Word. Let Him be God. He is rather good at it. Ask the Father to reveal the secret hopes and desires you have stored safely away. Then, with a trembling hand, give them to God and wait for Him to call you into the dance of your life. Only you can start the music. He is there, ready to take your hand and lead you into something so beautiful, so liberating, and so freeing that you will wonder if you really ever lived before.

No, God is not safe, but He is very, very good. Things done in secret get His attention. Unseen acts get the attention of the unseen God. The secret place in the life of the lifegiver, the inner sanctuary, is a life hidden in Christ. Every woman who wants to be noticed by the unseen God must embrace a lifestyle of unseen service, unseen prayer, unseen fasting, and unseen actions. This is what our loving and faithful God loves to reward! And sister, payday is sooner than we think.

> The Lord sends no one away empty except those who are full of themselves. Dwight L. Moody

Outward expression of an inward reality

It would have been easy to go straight to the how-tos of lifegiving. I love the fun side of lifegiving, in which the only books to read are four-color cookbooks and the only lists are for shopping. If that were all I shared, though, you would be able to create an outer beauty that is available to all hardworking do-gooders, but it would not be full of the inner beauty of the lifegiver. The beauty of the lifegiving woman radiates from her inner life, which is cultivated in the secret place of prayer and in deeds that are done in secret as unto God. This is the stuff of 1 Peter 3:3–4: "Your beauty should not come from outward adornment, such as braided hair and the wearing of gold jewelry and fine clothes. Instead, it should be that of your inner self, the unfading beauty of a gentle and quiet spirit, which is of great worth in God's sight."

God is highly interested in our inner life, so we should be too. The world wants us to believe that life is all about appearances. While the outer expressions of beauty and hospitality and friendship can and should have a wonderful appearance, true beauty is more than what the physical eye can perceive. It is not a façade covering over hurt, pain, and anger. Lifegiving is not done with an expectation for accolades. The motivations of the lifegiving woman are fueled by the inner life she is cultivating in the secret place with Christ Himself, the ultimate Lifegiver.

part two

The Lifegiving Lifestyle

chapter six

home The Lifegiving Home

Where we love is
home, home that our
feet may leave, but
not our hearts.
Oliver Wendell Holmes

Lifegiving women are compelled to raise life above mere existence. We know that in order to nurture, love, and care for others, we must thrive, not just survive! We are motivated to help others live beautiful lives. Jesus said in John 10:10, "I have come that they may have life, and that they may have it more abundantly" (NKJV). This is life that is excessive, greater, extreme. This is over-the-top living, as I like to say. Jesus did not just come to help us get by. He came to give us more than we can handle, so much that we cannot help but give it away.

Look again at John 10:10. Before Jesus gave the promise of abundant life, He warned us that realizing this divine life would be a battle. It would be a lifelong war with the thief and destroyer, Satan. Jesus contrasted the devil's destruction with His lifegiving intent. In this age, the world is fraught with death, destruction, and stealing. Jesus told us these are the works of the devil. Christ came not only to destroy death and the works of Satan, but He also came to replace these with His lifegiving eternal work.

Every time we go in His name and bring His life into a new situation, we continue Christ's work, whether to our own children when they come home from school or to starving children in a foreign land. To bring life is a beautiful thing. To be a lifegiver is to live a beautiful life. In a foreign land, a cheerful, Christ-kissed countenance is a feast to the eyes of the dying. A warm blanket provided by relief workers brings comfort to an estranged ethnic group as much as a quilt made by grandma brings comfort to your child.

The crowning virtue of love is at the heart of all lifegiving. Love naturally compels us as women to beautify. Love leads us to make the ordinary everydayness of life into something extraordinary. Creating places of beauty in our homes can do just that.

Feeding souls as we give life in and through our homes is not about having loads of money, expensive treasures, and perfect décor.

A stunning home, a beautifully set table, and a delicious meal are wonderful, without a doubt. But the ability to give love and to receive love in return has eternal value. And all this begins with God Himself, for God is not just loving—He is love.

> There's no place like home, there's no place like home!
> Dorothy in *The Wizard of Oz*

As lifegiving women we *can* raise life above mere existence. We have our sights set on more than just survival. We want to thrive and to help others do so too. All lifegiving begins in the home and flows from the home. Truly, home is our sanctuary on earth, our retreat from the world. Home is where we daily give our lives away. Home is where we teach golden truths with simple actions. Home is where we love deeply and give generously.

A God who loves beauty

God Himself has lifted up beauty as a testimony to His nature by creating a beautiful world. God loves beauty! He made a wonderful world for us to enjoy. All that is exquisite in Creation is a reflection of the nature of a glorious God. Romans 1:20 tells us, "From the time the world was created, people have seen the earth and sky and all that God made. They can clearly see his invisible qualities—his eternal power and divine nature. So they have no excuse whatsoever for not knowing God" (NLT).

Since we are the only part of Creation that bears God's image, it stands to reason that we would have a drive to express beauty— especially those of us fashioned in the garden. (Trust me—this is where Martha Stewart got the idea.)

Creating lifegiving beauty in our homes is not about big budgets and professional decorators. All of us have times, seasons, and lifestyles of frugality—thrift store shopping moments or even decades. But a simple twist of fabric around a window can make a room much more inviting. Placing a fresh flower arrangement on the table for dinner or lighting a few candles every night or turning on background music before you sit down to an everyday meal—these are the simple touches that can bring life to your home. *The focus must always be on the lifegiving intent.*

Beauty is the gift of God. Aristotle

No matter what we do out in the world, no matter what our lifestyle, almost all of us have a place we call home. Creating a lifegiving atmosphere in our home nurtures the souls of those who live there. Think about how much time you spend doing everyday rituals. Imagine capitalizing on these simple activities: eating, drinking, bathing, and sleeping. These daily rituals can offer us the gifts of rest, security, fellowship, refreshment, and connection. Because we do these activities every day, they are the perfect venue to bring forth simple, beautiful, daily offerings, like a gift we can unwrap each day.

As women, many of us feel our homes hold us captive to duty. As soon as we walk in the door, we are faced with work. We cannot see past the dishes in the sink, the crunching underfoot as we walk through the kitchen, the dirty toilet, the clothes strewn on the bedroom floor, not to mention the mountain of laundry waiting to be scaled. (How do I know this? Four kids, I tell you!) For many of us, home does not inspire possibilities for beauty; it represents work that is like a ball and chain we snap on when we cross the threshold.

Take heart, my lifegiving friend. Your home can be a place of beauty. You may not be able to make it to the summit of laundry mountain every week or keep every dirty dish clean, but your home

home

can be a place of refuge, solace, and love. Your home can be a haven for lifegiving. *Friend, what you need here is a new way of looking at an old idea.*

As lifegiving women, we must change the way we see things, and our view of home is one of the most important changes needed. You see, home is the place where you and your loved ones return after a long day out in the world. Whether you return to your home alone or you share your home with an active mob of kids, it can be a refuge amidst the storms of life, a safe zone from the battlefield of the marketplace, a warm spot after a chilling day at school.

Home, a taste of heaven

Jesus comforted His disciples in their final moments together by assuring them He was going to prepare a place for them. "Do not let your hearts be troubled. Trust in God; trust also in me. In my Father's house are many rooms; if it were not so, I would have told you. I am going there to prepare a place for you. And if I go and prepare a place for you, I will come back and take you to be with me that you also may be where I am" (John 14:1–3).

Scripture clearly teaches that what God is preparing is no heavenly shack! "No eye has seen, no ear has heard, no mind has conceived what God has prepared for those who love him" (1 Corinthians 2:9). Think of it. Beauty that you or I cannot even imagine, and girl, I can imagine a lot! Yes, I think God celebrates when we spiff things up down here on earth. It makes God smile when we rejoice in His creative beauty. Now that gets my creative juices flowing. Indeed, heaven will be filled with beauty and glory.

So how do we start to prepare our homes to be places of beauty, splendor, and holiness? Here are three simple principles for making your home a haven. It may not be the heaven God is preparing for us, but it can be a haven for us and for those we love.

87

1. Color it beautiful

When we were children, we were always asked, "What is your favorite color?" Maybe when you were young it was pink. Of course, I was always wild about violet. Maybe you love the blue of the cool sky, the red of a crisp apple, or the yellow of the warm sun. We all have feelings and memories about color.

Studies abound on the meaning and impact of color. Blue is said to be soothing, providing a sense of clarity and peace. Red represents passionate energy, orange brings joy and vitality, green represents harmony and healing, yellow fills a room with playful airiness, gold brings forth strength and prosperity, white conveys purity and holiness, and silver suggests perfect wisdom. And my all-time favorite color, purple, portrays royal leadership and priestly honor.

Color matters. Color evokes feelings. As Russian abstract painter Wassily Kandinsky said, "Colors directly influence the soul." Look at how God used splashes of tremendous color throughout all Creation. God must have chosen such stunning colors because He knew it would bring loveliness to our lives and glory to Himself. We too can learn how to use color to enhance our homes.

Different colors are "beautiful" to each of us, and our love of color transcends the latest fad. We should bring the colors into our individual homes that spell b-e-a-u-t-y to us. I like more masculine colors and earthy tones. Any given autumn day would be the perfect color palette for my home. Yet I go to my friend Phyllis's home and find the truer shades of red, yellow, and blue typical of her Norwegian background. My friend Jenny has plaids of red and white, sofas of denim blue, and lots of crisp white accents. Each person's choice is equally beautiful and uniquely comforting to her. The palette we choose for our homes is a backdrop for the mood and the emotion we will experience each day.

None of us has to live with white walls! Even when Butch and I lived in an apartment, I painted the walls. When we moved out, I just painted them all back to lackluster white. Now, I understand that some of you love white. And yes, that is okay, too. But when you add touches of color to your shades of white, you will notice a difference in the mood and comfort of your home. No matter where you live, you can splash color around with paint, fabrics, tablecloths, and even throws.

The purest and most thoughtful minds are those which love color the most. John Ruskin

Paint is the least expensive and most wonderful way to bring color into your home. Pick one shade for the kitchen, one for the living area, yet another for the entrance. When people come into my home, the most common comment is, "Wow, I love how you have used such strong colors in your home." When we see someone else use color in a dramatic way, we feel more confident to try it ourselves.

If you do not know where to start, consult a decorator or a friend. Flip through magazines or books at the library to find decorating tips. Discover how you can use several shades of color in harmony throughout your home. Go to the paint store and collect as many color samples as you want. Spread them out on the floor and organize what colors to put in each room of your house. When we moved to our home in Colorado, I painted several colors directly on the walls and asked everyone who came into my home to vote for their favorite shade. I even kept a tally of which color was running in first place. In my opinion, color belongs everywhere.

You can even paint your ceiling. When I painted my living room ceiling brick leather red, Butch's response was something noncommittal like, "Well, honey, it sure is different. I mean, really nice. You know, different. Very unique . . . but I trust you!" I just smile when people come over and rave about my red ceiling. Every room, every wall, is fair game for color.

Think of all the shades of color on the earth. There is the aquamarine of the Caribbean, the reds, oranges, yellows, and purples of a dramatic sunset, the deep red of a garnet buried in a mountain, the salmon-colored rock in the West, the rich lavish greens in the Midwest, even the bright colors of the Tucan parrot. I have painted on my family room wall a verse that declares the magnificence of our Pikes Peak view. "The heavens declare the glory of God; the skies proclaim the work of his hands" (Psalm 19:1). Friend, go out and glimpse the original, and then copy away. God will not mind.

2. Comfortable furnishings

Some of us can go to a furniture store and pick out everything we want, furnishing our homes in short order. (I have not met someone like this yet, but I am sure you are out there.) Most of us must pick carefully and save up for special purchases, often improvising in the meantime. Often we can find tag sale items and thrift store tables and chairs that approximate what we see in popular home décor magazines. All of us can work at filling our homes with lovely and comfortable furnishings.

> Decorating is the art of arranging beautiful things comfortably.
> Ruby Ross Wood

Again, talking with a friend or looking through some magazines will help. I love to look through magazines and see how decorators have arranged the furniture in the model rooms. Arranging on angles always creates a more interesting space. Instead of putting your couch against the wall, put it on an angle in the middle of the room or the corner. Decorating books can give you many new ideas. These designers are paid thousands of dollars to get the arrangement and mood just right. Save yourself a lot of headaches by just copying their ideas.

Pillows and throw blankets bring coziness into a family or living area. Create corners of comfort you look forward to visiting for twenty minutes of reading or relaxation or for a cup of tea with a friend. Tamra has many little seating areas throughout her house. When I stop by, she always says, "Well, today let's sit . . . here!" It adds a fun and creative element to our times together.

Start where you spend the most time, and make that area extra comfortable. For me, it is the kitchen (of course). Perhaps for you it is your family room or bedroom. Wherever you and your family pass the most time, invest there first. You will be drawn to those places over and over again.

3. Come to your senses

In addition to the color scheme, furnishings, and home accessories, you can create a sensory experience in your home. Everyone loves good smells, delicious tastes, and the sounds of comforting or uplifting music ascending to the rafters. Sights, sounds, smells, and tastes are the stuff of sensory-therapy (cheaper than a therapist, too).

Scents have an incredible impact on our daily lives. Lavender provides a calming effect and is said to be good for insomnia. Cinnamon provides comfort and peace. Cloves help with memory and clarity. (I need more cloves in my life.) The scent and sight of roses provides a universal message of love and beauty, whereas pine and cedar are down-to-earth. A cup of chamomile tea brings relaxation and serenity, and garden-fresh mint brings clarity and freshness. These are all gifts that God has given to us for our enjoyment and healing.

Aroma has incredible power. Of all the five senses, only smell travels directly to the brain. When you smell vanilla, does it send you back to your mother's kitchen, a place that felt warm and safe to you? The smell of vinegar reminds me of hot summer pickling days with my mother in Minnesota. I still plug my nose just thinking about it. What about the smell of sawdust? My father was a carpenter and had his own shop in our basement. My sisters and I used to gather up the sawdust to make pies, cakes, and meatloaf. Just this year, my dad visited me in Colorado and lovingly made me some storage shelves in my basement. While he was sawing, visions of sawdust pies filled my happy thoughts! Smells evoke memories and experiences we associate with them.

> Of all earthly music, that which reaches farthest into heaven is the beating of a loving heart. Henry Ward Beecher

The senses are a venue through which we can experience life more beautifully. My daughter smelled the cinnamon I was putting in baked goods the other day and said, "Mom, that smells like Christmas." That made me smile, because, after all, Christmas is her favorite time of year. Know that every time you bake or light a favorite candle or fill your home with delicious smells, you are giving your children the gift of happy smells and beautiful experiences. Trust me, your home is not always meant to be pristine and orderly. Give yourself and your children a break and bake away, real flour and all.

After reading through the three principles of making your home a beautiful place, some of you may feel inspired to begin. Others of you may be thinking, "But I am not creative! I can't decorate!" How can you use color and décor to supply the backdrop for creating a beautiful life at home when you feel so ill-equipped? You can learn, and you can find help. We all gain confidence by trying and growing in our success. You must start simply but simply start. That is one of my favorite life mottos.

Some people are born with an extra helping of creativity. The rest of us can cultivate it. You can learn to produce beauty by training yourself. Or you can hire a professional, funds permitting, who can help you discover your personal preferences. Ask a friend who has this talent for help. Take her to lunch for "pay." I have been taken to lunch many times, and I really enjoy it. If your friend is naturally creative, she will consider it a joy to serve you, and she will be flattered that you asked.

This is not a book about interior design. And living a beautiful life is certainly not the sum total of our furnishings and window fashions. Yet the environment we create can either be an asset or a detriment to our lives as lifegivers. Just think of the possibilities for inner beauty coming forth in a place of outer beauty—beauty as *you* define it for your home.

See new possibilities in everyday activities

Every year when summer ends, we send our young children back to school. This is an annual event. Usually it is sad for the kids, though maybe a little happy for moms. Why not turn this time into a cause for celebration? This year Tamra threw an "End of the Summer Party" with balloons and brightly colored tablecloths and plates. She placed an inexpensive gift in a colorful little gift bag at each child's place. She bought a chocolate cake with a smiley face and a pair of plastic sunglasses for eyes. What a celebration!

Every Valentine's Day, Tamra makes breakfast with red pancakes, red juice served in champagne glasses, festive red plates and napkins, and a card and little gift bag. She found another way to say "I love you" in unforgettable terms. These inexpensive ideas take life from simple living to abundant living!

My children love to have a neighborhood "Feed the Birds" party each fall. We gather up fallen pinecones, spread peanut butter on them, and roll them in birdseed. We string popcorn and cranberries. I bring out hot cocoa with cinnamon sticks, and we party! It is great fun and very little work.

Most of us celebrate birthdays, anniversaries, and the major holidays. But we can look at many regular events as opportunities for celebration, and they do not have to be elaborate or expensive. Try "Teatime with Mom." Prepare a little plate of cookies, let your son or daughter or a neighbor child pick out a special china tea cup, boil the water, pick a cozy corner in the house, and voilá! You have made an after-school snack time special with only twenty minutes to prepare, share, and clean up. If you do this once a week or once a month, you will have a new ritual that will never be forgotten. Look into each other's eyes over the teacups as you sip, and you have touched the heart and warmed the soul of someone you love. My girls are now teenagers, and they *still* love having tea with Mom. (And now they make it and serve me!)

Go to the well

Let us not forget to nurture our own souls. The lifegiver must continue to refill her tank too. This cannot be overstated. We must do this by turning our daily rituals into times when we can find refreshment and solitude. Every real giver must first be a good receiver. We must have an awareness that we need to stop, pull back, and be filled up. We must *be* and not just *do*. This is an intentional act. It will never happen unless you choose to do it. Yes, taking time to be alone is often much easier said than done. Of course, it would be much easier if you lived with a maid, nanny, cook, and a chauffeur. For most of us, though, this is just wishful thinking. The demands keep coming, and too often we live in react mode. Without intending to, we respond to the most demanding and miss out on the most important. This is a terrible snare because it costs us so much. Then, when we most desperately need it, we do not have life to give because we have been drained dry. We must learn to go to the well for lifegiving refreshment.

Make a point of putting yourself in places that help you slow down, tune out the clamor and listen to the quiet. Emily Barns

---

Quiet times of prayer and reflection are crucial for lifegiving. We must receive from the lifegiving well of Christ Himself if we are to continue refreshing others. It is so important that we have this *rhythm* of giving and receiving in our lives. If you do not have this, sister, start simply, but simply start.

Bubbles away!

The bath. Does that seem like a rare luxury for you? With a few small tweaks in your daily routine, it can be an everyday time when you can relax and reflect. I admit, bath time is a daily staple in my often hectic life.

Carve out twenty minutes for a bath close to your bedtime. Lock the door, light a few sweet-smelling candles, fill the tub with hot water and some fragrant bath salts, or keep a bath cleansing gel on hand. Splurge and get a bath pillow to press on to the end of the tub so you can sit back, relax, unwind, and just reflect on your day. Breathe prayer in and out to your Lord, or read a few pages of a favorite book, or listen to strains of a favorite classic composer in the background. Some of my sweetest times in worship have been while I was soaking in a hot tub, quiet, alone, reflective. This daily ritual has calmed and refreshed me time and time again.

My son, Samuel, understood this. I still remember a particularly stressful day, when I was snapping at everyone, growling at everything, and generally making PMS look good. That evening, Sam came downstairs and said, "Mom, I have a surprise for you!" My first grumpy thought was, *Is this another mess I am going to have to clean up?* Guilt got the best of me, and I followed him upstairs, blindfolded at his request.

As I walked into my bedroom, I was indeed met with a surprise. Sam had lit some candles, run a bubble bath, and filled a glass of sparkling water for me. Next to the rose on my pillow was a handwritten note telling me five reasons why I was a great mom. I felt so touched (and guilty). I told him how much this meant to me and how I really needed this. To this he replied, "Mom, I've been thinking. You know, when Dad is gone, I know it can get hard on you sometimes. You just need a little extra loving. Yep, while Dad is away I think I need to be your 'foster husband'!"

That was life to me! When I asked Sam how he got such a thoughtful idea he replied, "I saw Dad do it for you." Friend, they are watching, learning, and growing in the art of lifegiving.

The idle man does not know what it is to enjoy rest. Albert Einstein

That evening, I stepped out refreshed, warmed, and ready for the next phase of my evening. My whole family benefited because of it. Women, we need this! As Pascal said, "A little thing comforts us because a little thing afflicts us." Take a moment and soothe those little things.

Come on, give it a try. Instead of flying through a shower, fill the tub and linger long enough to cleanse your soul from the troubles and stresses of the day. Release your prayers to the God who cares for all that concerns you, and warm your body and soul. Make the ordinary extraordinary.

Make every day a vacation

I am convinced that one of life's greatest blessings is the ability to find joy and pleasure in our often mundane daily efforts. Is it the expensive, time-consuming travel that brings true contentment? If you were to look at my travel record, you would find that just the opposite is true for me. This lifegiving woman often comes home more exhausted, crabbier, and most assuredly more broke than when she left! So what do we want from our vacations anyway? Lost luggage, Montezuma's revenge, and daunting credit card bills? I think not.

What we often long for when we plan a vacation is a reprieve from the stresses of daily life and a break from the routine. You can actually build a sense of "vacation" into your daily routine and save money in the process. Coming home can be the best trip around.

Plan what really nurtures your soul—ten minutes to read the paper or thirty minutes with your favorite novel. Take a walk on a beautiful day (or on a rainy day, for that matter). Cut fresh flowers to grace your table. Plant flower bulbs and sink your fingers into the rich earth. Sister, what is it that brings you a sense of serenity and pure enjoyment? What do you really long to do? Where do you find a respite, a place of renewal and joy? As lifegiving women we must change our focus and not just be led along by the things that demand our attention. Truly, the simple pleasures bring contentment and joy.

Do freedom and release come from stepping onto the sandy beaches pictured in the four-color resort brochures we pick up at the travel agency? Our hearts may sing at the thought of letting a cruise ship take us away. But the opportunity to squish our toes in the sand may never come, or it may be a long way off. Often these dreams of the future rob us of enjoying the present. We must see the everyday-ness of life in a new way. Dear friend, if we have eyes to see the possibilities in everyday life, we can often experience what vacations promise but so seldom deliver.

I have a good friend who is continually stressed out. Her constant comment is, "If I could just get two weeks away from everything, to relax, things would be so much better." She has never come close to taking two weeks off. In fact, when she does take one week off, all she can think about is what she is missing at work. Two weeks may never come, but twenty minutes of transformed focus could completely change your outlook on life.

Let go and live

Alexandra Stoddard explores the idea of living each day to the fullest in her book *Living a Beautiful Life*. She explains that 5 percent of our living time translates into a few outstanding special events. Ninety-five percent of our lives are lived daily, the mundane routine we often overlook. But life is not dress rehearsal. Single days experienced fully add up to a lifetime lived deeply and well.[4]

Today is your life, not yesterday or tomorrow. We only have today. Clearly we are instructed by Christ to live one day at a time, for it is all we can possibly embrace this side of reality. (Read Luke 12:16–21 and James 4:13–14.) God wants us to live one faith-filled day at a time. He understands it is all we can hope to handle; it is all we can clearly see. Receive every moment as a gift from God's loving hands. Resist the temptation to live for tomorrow or for a better time. Accept today from the Lord, and live it fully.

You may have noticed that this is not a chapter on "Ten Steps to

an Immaculate Home" or "How to Organize Your Cleaning Schedule."
You will have to go back to the bookstore for that one. (And trust me,
I will never be writing a book on those topics!) I hope you will enjoy
this message a bit more. Sit back, relax, leave those dishes in the
sink, and take time to enjoy life all around you. Capture a moment
with your loved ones—a moment that could have been stolen by the
natural busyness of the day. Those everyday moments have the potential of becoming lifegiving opportunities. Some of the best memories
in life begin when we say yes to surprising moments—*the moments
we do not plan ahead for but moments for which we make room.*
Does that sound good so far? I thought it might.

Reflections on a beautiful life

Will you go with me to the end of your life and look back? What really
matters cannot always be seen in advance. Too often, we are plagued
with time-stealing thoughts such as the following:

"If only we could have children."

"When the kids are gone, we will finally be able to . . . "

"If my husband ever changes . . . "

"If I had a husband . . . "

"Someday I will have a career I've longed for . . . "

"When I have more money . . . "

"When we have a house . . . "

"If we could just have a bigger house . . . "

Some of these yearnings are the inevitable result of living in a
materialistic world, while others may be valid unfulfilled longings. Yet
I have learned that merely driving toward the future can keep us from
living well in the present. It can blind us toward missed opportunities.
We waste so much time with endeavors and desires that never add
value to our lives or to the lives of those we love.

Ecclesiastes 7:2 tells us, "It is better to go to a house of mourning than to go to a house of feasting, for death is the destiny of every man; the living should take this to heart." Why should lifegiving women visit the house of mourning? When a follower of Christ dies, we often find valuable lessons when we look back on a life well lived. We are reminded that life is shorter than we think and that the small daily acts of lifegiving can add up to untold eternal treasures. I visited that house of mourning this year, and it has profoundly changed my perspective on life.

> If we really think that home is elsewhere, and that this life is a wandering to find home, why should we not look forward to the arrival? C. S. Lewis

The month Tatiana came home from Russia and Mikia was born, I received another daughter of sorts. She was a beautiful, eighteen-year-old, vibrant, Christian girl living in a very difficult situation in Mexico. We learned about her through a good friend. After speaking with her and her family, we decided she was to be a part of our family.

Viviana came to stay with us one week before Butch came home from Russia with Tatiana. I still remember picking her up at the airport. She was so darling and young and spoke so little English. In one month I gained a daughter who spoke Russian and one who spoke Spanish, while I lived with a pocket dictionary in my hand.

Vivi lived with us for almost two years. She was my right hand. We had no idea she would be in our home for such an extended period of time when she came. She became more than just a daughter to me; she became my dearest friend. Her brother Victor also made a journey to our home. He was a tall, handsome man, terribly protective of his sister. The two of them become a central part of our family's wild and wonderful times. Those were the Vivi and Victor days, which are some of my children's happiest memories.

When I think of Vivi, I think of simple things. Her passion was to lovingly serve and not merely to be served. I clearly remember her loving the children, playing, and laughing. She taught the children how to dance unto the Lord, tambourines and all. She was a beautiful, pure worshipper, the kind that our heavenly Father seeks.

We had wild cooking times together. She cooked me her favorite Mexican dishes (hot, hot, hot!), and I cooked my American ones (boring, boring, boring). We talked for long hours about the kind of man she hoped to marry, the children she would hold, the life she asked God to give her. She longed to have a big family and thought adoption was the most beautiful way to build a family. She picked out countries that sounded interesting to adopt from, always finishing with her beloved Mexico.

> Remember that when you leave this earth, you can take nothing that you have received . . . but only what you have given: a full heart enriched by honest service, love, sacrifice and courage.
>
> Francis of Assisi

Butch said he knew of no one who loved our children like Vivi. She was there through Tatiana's hard adjustment and Mikia's baby years. She was there rocking Samuel to sleep. She took Mackenzie on bike rides and told her what a wonderful big sister she was and why that was so important. Vivi was the older sister Mackenzie always wanted. Just having Vivi in our home brought us life abundant. It was a life well lived, full of simple moments we gladly shared together, moments too quickly gone.

Last year I received a very distressed phone call from Victor. He told us that Viviana was very sick. She had a tumor on her ovary, and the doctors were very concerned. I felt frantic and called Vivi immediately. As she and I talked, she told me the seriousness of her condition. The doctors were concerned that her cancer had spread into several areas of her body. As she spoke with unnerving peace, my mind raced. I felt tormented with fear and anxiety. This was my child, my sister, my friend. This was terribly wrong. She was only twenty-seven years old, a beautiful lifegiving woman, a true picture of the bride of Christ, pure, set apart, and faithful.

Before I left for Dallas two weeks later to see Vivi, the children came up with a wonderful idea. They decided to make a special picture book for Vivi. We went on a search through literally thousands of pictures. But what we really discovered were memories, beautiful recollections of our life together. As the children chose the pictures and wrote letters telling her their favorite "Vivi memories," we laughed, told stories, and remembered how she had made our home a happy place.

As my youngest daughter Mikia was reading me her letter and showing me pictures she had discovered of her and Vivi, she began to cry. With salty tears rolling down her pink cheeks, she said, "Mama, how will I ever smile again without Vivi? She called me 'my little presioso.' She is all mixed up in my heart. How will I tell my heart she is not here?"

I thought I would dissolve into nothingness. I was experiencing my own grief, but the grief of my children was overwhelming to me. I answered, "Mikia, the reason Vivi feels all mixed up in your heart is because she is. All the happy memories—like how you learned to read *together,* her homemade birthday piñatas, snuggling late at night, making backyard adventures—all become a part of what your heart is today. Vivi will never leave our hearts; she has become part of them."

Two weeks passed, and I traveled to Dallas to see Vivi. When I walked in the room, I saw her lying quietly on her bed, obviously very sick. I walked over to hold her. She looked up at me with a smile that changed everything in that room, including me. She had the life of Christ within her. Even as her body was wasting away, her inner spirit was strong.

She loved the picture book and touched each picture as if to live the memory over again. Carefully she read each letter, making comments and sweet reflections. We cried, laughed, and prayed. I told her what a gift she had been to me during such a hard time in my life. Her simple ways produced such beautiful love in our home.

> At the moment of death, we will not be judged by the amount of work we have done but by the weight of love we have put into our work. This love should flow from self-sacrifice, and it must be felt to the point of hurting. Mother Teresa

Moments later a nurse came in to tell us the medical prognosis. Time seemed to stop. The nurse said that Vivi had a 10 percent chance of being alive in two years. It felt unreal. Even then, as she heard what would come unless God chose to supernaturally heal her body, she took my hand and tenderly squeezed it. She said she was at peace and confidently knew she was, after all, Christ's bride. "Do not fear, sister. My Lord is in control, and I trust Him. Yes, I have received such a rich life."

Rich? I thought. *Hard* was more like it. Painful memories she had to overcome. Financial hardships. Unmet dreams. She was a promise in the making. *Rich* was not what came to mind. But then again, that was the perfect picture of Vivi. She continually set her eyes on what was eternal, what really mattered, what would last.

Ten days later I received a phone call from my dear friend Autumn. All I could hear was her sobbing. "She's gone, Tammy. She's gone. Her Bridegroom called her home just moments ago. Vivi was His bride. The wedding dance has begun, and she was ready to go. You know she was ready to go."

I wept. The ache felt unbearable. I cried for my loss, for my children, and for her family. But I never cried for her. You see, she was a woman who lived life well. Oh yes, I would miss the simple things about her—her touch, her words, her smile. It is interesting how much we miss the simple things in life when they elude us. A messy kitchen or a costly bill pales in comparison to the loss of someone you love. Perspective is everything.

Someone once said, "When you love, give it everything you've got, and when you've reached your limit, give it more and forget the pain of it, because as you face your death it is only the love you have given and received which will count. All the rest—the accomplishments and struggles, the fights—will be forgotten in your reflection, and if you have loved well, then it will have been worth it, and the joy of it will last you through the end, but if you have not, death will always come too soon and be too terrible to face." As I sat there I was reminded of my desire to find those moments when love was freely given and freely received. The moments I could no longer create. Moments that would become the mortar that held together the memories I now carried. I knew then I could only draw from the well I had already filled. And at that moment I was glad the well was full.

You see, friend, the clock of regret waits for no one. A moment in the making is what we are promised. Our lives, our homes, our love speak volumes to those around us. Measure the time. Weigh your choices. Live well. It is the gift you will someday leave behind.

Tonight the dishes will wait, candles will be lit, and memories will be made in my spiritual house. Tonight we will share simple pleasures that make everyday life beautiful.

chapter seven

Lifegiving in Friendships

friendships

> Friendships are
> gathered and tied
> with heartstrings.
>
> *Anonymous*

All of us value intimate, loving friendships that grow over time, remain strong through the good and bad times, and bring peace to our often chaotic lives. As women, we long for true friends to celebrate life's little victories with us and to weather the difficult storms that will inevitably come. Loving care, intimate understanding, a deep and abiding connection is what we yearn for—even ache for. There is something simply wonderful about a friend who will stick with us, see the best in us, and encourage us along the journey. This is the most satisfying of all friendships. These are the rich, rewarding, satisfying friendships that seem so rare.

My friends are my estate. Emily Dickinson

You see, I believe women need women, cradle to the grave. Today, possibly more than ever before, women need women to stand by their sides, holding up each other's arms and speaking courage into each other's souls. When the pain of life violently buffets us, our lifegiving, life-sustaining friendships consistently become a loving safety net that pulls us back to a safe shore.

In a time of crisis, we almost instinctively reach out for a good and faithful friend, a friend who knows us, hears us, and loves us. This good friend can help provide us with the insight and support needed to pass the test of disappointment, misery, and confusion. When the choice is clear, women will always choose to have lifelong, lifegiving friendships rather than autonomy and independence.

We need these trusted female friendships to become a part of our lifegiving garden. Like perennial flowers, the blooms of these friendships grow richer and more rewarding with each passing season. Our friends, like flowers, display an array of beautiful fragrances and hues. Cultivating a garden of lifegiving friendship is a labor of love filled with rich purpose and significance.

So the question begs to be asked, "If this lifegiving garden is so essential for our well-being, then why do we as women often hold back from giving ourselves to one another in loving friendship?"

For some of us, the answer is that we have misdirected our desire for female friendships. Some women expect their husbands to satisfy their need for friendship, companionship, and conversation. And while many husbands may be good at playing those roles, they are not meant to totally fill that void in their wives' hearts. Very often, when women expect (and even demand) that their husbands take the place of any female friends, they put undue stress on their marriage. Sister, you may have the greatest husband in the world, but trust me in this—you need your girlfriends too!

SIMPLE LIFEGIVING . . . MAKING NEW FRIENDS

Press past your fear and reach out to a new acquaintance . . .

- Ask her for her phone number and actually call her sometime the following week.

- Invite her over for tea.

- If she is a struggling mom ask if you can watch her kids for her for two hours so she can do uninterrupted errands.

- Take her family a meal if you know she needs a break.

- Sit by her at a church function or invite her to sit with you and introduce her to your other friends.

- Ask her and her husband over for dessert one evening. Plan to ask them three questions so they can share their story with you and you won't have to worry about what to say—let them do the talking!

For others of us, the answer is that the cost of cultivating this garden of friendship has been too great in the past. We have been hurt or betrayed by someone we intimately trusted with personal information. We have been lied to, lied about, and left holding a rotten bouquet of well-meaning intentions. Trust in these relationships has been costly, loyalty scarce. We have cried tears of indifference and bled the pain of rejection. Why, then, should we even consider revisiting the process of friendship?

Simply put, because the beautiful blossoms of lifegiving friendship are worth the effort and risk! This is a simple but life-changing principle. You need to do the hard work of tilling the soil and planting and cultivating the seed if you want to enjoy a garden of friendship.

Don't wait for things to happen; make them happen yourself. Don't wait for a friend to ask you to spend an afternoon together; invite her first. Alexandra Stoddard

You have to take risks. You may need to put behind you past ideas of female relationships and be willing to step out into new territory. Will be you discouraged at times? Yes! Will you be disappointed in the friends you are working hard to love and bless? Oh yes! Will you wonder if it is worth the fear, the hurt, and the uncertainty? Yes, yes, yes.

All of us have seasons of dormancy in our friendship gardens. These are times when we do not find the friends we desire. We struggle to feel connected, understood, and loved. But even these times deepen the meaning of friendship.

What I am sharing with you has changed my life and at times saved it. Through the many twists and turns in my journey, enduring, patient, lifegiving friends have come to tutor me and hold me up. They have taught me the enduring love of my heavenly Father and His great and mighty care for me as a woman. They have brought laughter and joy when I most needed it. These women have been a well that I run to when my lifegiving cup is empty. There is no relationship that holds the key to meet all your needs or desires. Only God Himself can do this. But God uses our friends to pour His comfort, His wisdom, His joy, His mercy, and His grace into our lives.

No man is wise enough by himself.   Titus Maccius Platius

Female friends are God's promise keepers to each other. We are the literal, living, breathing, pulsating body of Christ here on earth. God honors His promises by giving us the privilege of fulfilling them. When a single mother sits in her home at night, alone and over-whelmed, and she reads Joshua 1:5, "I will never leave you nor forsake you," how does she know this to be true? She knows when a life-giving woman presses into her life and her isolation. She knows when a lifegiving friend knocks on her door with a homemade meal. She knows when her lifegiving friend offers to watch her kids while she runs errands, or better yet, when her lifegiving friend arranges for someone to stay with her kids so she can take her friend out for lunch. It is our tangible, practical actions that preach the gospel of Jesus to the world. St. Francis said, "Preach the gospel at all times. If necessary, use words." We are never more like Christ than when we're loving, sacrificing, and giving our lives away. We must take responsibility for one another, for in doing so, we embody God's promises to each other.

Each friendship is a different flower in our friendship garden. It is a garden of comfort and encouragement, celebrating a vast variety of all colors, shapes, and sizes. As George Santayana said, "Friendship is almost always the union of a part of one mind with a part of another;

people are friends in spots." These lifegiving friendships, bound together, create a rewarding and magnificent bouquet.

Cultivating lifegiving friendships

When we moved to Colorado after living in Dallas for thirteen years, I knew I needed to press in to new relationships. I was willing to do this, regardless of what it cost me, because I knew how much I needed female friends close by. In the process, and in each new friendship I have made, I have noticed a similar pattern of growth in the development of friendships.

Respect . . . is the appreciation of the separateness of another person, of the ways in which he or she is unique. Annie Gottlieb

The Honeymoon Season

The honeymoon season is always an enjoyable season but is very short-lived and often lacking in depth. When you meet someone you want to become friends with, you move from acquaintance to friendship. Often we take this step because we are drawn to this new person. Perhaps we share a passion for the same things or we enjoy one another's personalities. At other times we just know God has brought us together for a purpose, and we are taken up with the excitement of what He plans to do. In any event, there is a natural focus on the positive qualities that draw us together.

The Disappointment Season

Then comes the disappointment season. It is easy to love people who are easy to love. Loving one another only when we look lovely really costs us nothing! If we stop at that phase, we generally do not appreciate these relationships like those we have labored over and invested in.

SIMPLE LIFEGIVING . . . OVERCOMING THE DISAPPOINTMENT PHASE

Overcome the disappointment phase in a friendship with one of the following acts of kindness . . .

- Write a note to her and recall what you appreciate about her and what brought you together as friends originally.

- Ask a few friends to meet you for lunch, and include the friend you are disappointed in, even though you may not feel like it.

- Give her a big hug the next time you see her instead of avoiding her. Press in—don't pull back.

- Drop flowers on her porch and leave her a voice mail that there is a sweet-smelling surprise on her doorstep.

- Take her a pie or a cake or homemade cookies to "sweeten" her day.

The disappointment phase is a necessary season for every enduring friendship. It is the time when people are difficult to love. In this season we experience unmet expectations, harsh judgmental words, jealousy, and unforgiveness. We see the sin in others—and they see ours! We grapple with the fallout of that sin, and we make a choice to either do it God's way or our way. Of course, God's way will cost us something. It requires us to repent of our pride and our self-righteousness and to lay down our rights. But the ways of God are always better than ours. And they bring forth true life. If we choose to follow God's path to selfless, loving relationships, we will move beautifully into the next season. This is the lifegiving season of friendship.

The Lifegiving Season

The lifegiving season is where true and abiding relationships are nurtured. The hallmark of this type of friendship is *love*. Through sacrificial love we clearly see the power of lifegiving. King David said, "I will not sacrifice to the LORD my God burnt offerings that cost me nothing" (2 Samuel 24:24). Lifegiving friendships will always cost you something. But they are well worth the price!

> To love and be loved is to feel the sun from both sides. Anonymous

Celebrating life together

Sometimes you will be the wellspring of water for a friend who is going through a desert experience. Other times you will be the one who is being refreshed. Lifegiving women, in the hand of a loving God, become instruments of His sufficiency, hope, and healing in the lives of others.

My fortieth birthday celebration illustrates this so clearly in my mind. Age has always been an enemy to us as women. How true it was for me! Unfortunately, there was no stopping this biological clock, and the stroke of forty was about to chime. I have never been one to plan big parties to mark my own aging process. But I decided this birthday called for a celebration to ward off depression! For a year I planned, saved, and dreamed of a glorious way to greet forty.

One evening, while I gazed at Hawaiian brochures, the perfect celebration came to mind. I imagined a quiet, sunny beach experience complete with rest, laughter, and good food. So I strategized how to sell my husband on this grand plan. This was going to be tricky. The good news is that I have a very generous husband who knew that I was feeling a bit stressed about turning forty. When the warm Hawaiian getaway was presented, he was thrilled. He said he would love to go to Hawaii, and he felt it would be a perfect way for us to ring in my fortieth.

This is where things went from tricky to sticky. I was planning to take this Hawaiian vacation, not with him, but with four of my closest friends! Do not misinterpret this. I always enjoy time away with my husband. But this was different. I felt the need to be with dear friends for this milestone birthday.

Several of these women have known me for decades through many of life's challenges—and love me in spite of it. These are godly women, two of whom I had the privilege of leading to the Lord many years ago. These are fun-loving women who would laugh with me. These are women of depth who have felt the sting of life's deepest losses and have still remained tender and passionate. These are life-giving women.

After the shock wore off, Butch asked, "So what you are asking me is, will I watch the children, walk the dog, pay for the vacation, and not go?" I just smiled. To his great credit, Butch said yes! And not only was he willing to let me go, he genuinely wanted me to have a great time.

The greatest happiness in life is the conviction that we are loved, loved for ourselves, or rather, loved in spite of ourselves. Victor Hugo

What is so amazing about this Hawaiian birthday memory is the deep connection we all experienced with one another. This fellowship is a common denominator in the one-on-one friendships that I have with each of these women. Yet I was amazed to find us all united in this same love with one another. Turning forty could have been a depressing birthday, but instead it brought glorious memories shared with friends. These friends have moved with me through the honeymoon and disappointment phases and on into the lifegiving phase of friendship. Each of us will cherish these memories for the rest of our lives.

Each night in Hawaii, we focused on my individual friendship with one of the four women. We shared how God had brought us together and how it had defined our lives in powerful ways. We laughed about the unique joys and trials of friendship. We shared our journey of growing as godly wives and mothers and how we were discovering what it means to be whole and healed women. These conversations meant so much to me.

Weathering the storms

The story of my fortieth birthday in Hawaii with friends is not complete without telling you what I experienced one night. That evening we focused on my friendship with Maryjo. Of all the women there, I had known her longest—twenty-eight years. In many ways, Maryjo is like a younger sister to me. When I shared the Lord with her at the age of twelve, she joyfully received His love. The seed of the gospel fell on the good soil of her heart, took root, and continues to produce good fruit. Maryjo is a true, genuine, and kind woman. She always sees the best in others. Because I was her "older sister" in the journey of life, she often came to my well for a drink or two. I loved supporting and encouraging her (and often felt that I was the one being refreshed!).

> Faithful are the wounds of a friend; deceitful are the kisses of an enemy.

Then, when I went through the bitter and painful divorce in my early twenties, all of this changed. As I have shared, this barren winter of my life brought deep pain and regret. During that season, I withdrew from most of my friends and family because of the shame and disgrace that I felt. It was a lonely journey that took me further and kept me longer then I ever thought possible. And one of the consequences of my choices was the hurt experienced by those who knew and loved me—including Maryjo.

After my divorce, Maryjo felt very unsettled. Her friend, her example, her Christian mentor, had fallen. The one who introduced her to Christ, the sister who seemed strong, evangelistic, and full of the grace of God had failed her. Maryjo had to make a painful discovery. The tower of strength she had leaned on had serious foundational cracks and was no longer a place of security and strength. My choices made her question God.

'Tis sweet to stammer one letter of the Eternal's language; on earth it is called forgiveness. Henry Wadsworth Longfellow

---

Those difficult days left Maryjo with an agonizing choice. "Do I press into God, or do I leave my eyes on the woman who first led me to Him?" The choice for her was clear. She pressed into God. The memory of this period of my life still holds much sadness. Now, as I listened to her sweet tribute and thought about our years of friendship, I was reliving the impact my choices had on one so dear and close to me. What grief I felt!

I knew that I had been forgiven of my sin. I believed 1 John 1:9. "If we confess our sins, he is faithful and just and will forgive us our sins and purify us from all unrighteousness." I had confessed my sin, and I knew I was cleansed, as Isaiah 1:18 promises. I had found forgiveness and cleansing in Jesus and had been restored, pardoned, and washed clean. Despite all of this, the hard truth was that I had to finally face, years later, how my sin had wounded a dear friend.

Though I had been forgiven, I had not dealt with the impact my sin had on others. The fear of facing that pain kept me running. I saw that pain as the enemy rather than seeing it as a path to freedom in Christ. Truth is your greatest enemy until you allow it to become your closest friend.

Friendship doubles our joys and halves our grief. Dolley Madison

Instinctively, I think both Maryjo and I knew this dynamic was in play in our friendship for many years. The stain of my guilt was clearly visible to us both, yet we never spoke of what we saw. I struggled with it over and over again through the years that followed. I did everything I could to elude the pain, and it was exhausting. Honestly, in quiet moments of soul-searching over the years, I did not fully believe that God could bring life from the death sown by this sinful woman.

But that night in Hawaii I learned again the lifegiving principle of John 12:24. "I tell you the truth, unless a kernel of wheat falls to the ground and dies, it remains only a single seed. But if it dies, it produces many seeds." There in the presence of lifegiving friends, Jesus was about to take years of shame, bury it, and grow new life again.

As Maryjo gave a lovely tribute to me, never even speaking of the past, something in me started to break. Powerful waves of guilt and shame swept over me, and I felt terrified. My past mistakes engulfed me in fresh waves. I was gasping for air as I sought to process the pain and disappointment that I felt and that others had felt in me. It was the outpouring of bitter grief and shame I had carried for seventeen years. All I could grasp was how I had failed her, how I had failed the Lord, how I had failed so many others I loved. The waters of regret nearly overwhelmed me.

Emotionally, I was the seed, pushed into the ground, into the dark place beneath the earth. "Unless a kernel of wheat falls to the ground and dies, it remains only a single seed." The dying process had begun; real life was on the way.

I knew what God was calling me to do. I needed to confront the pain of this and ask Maryjo to forgive me. I longed to know the freedom that forgiveness offers. In reality, I needed to ask her for forgiveness more than she needed to forgive. I was grieved that I had put her in a spiritual wilderness. With my hands shaking and my eyes filled with tears, I owned the pain my sin had caused her. She quickly tried to free me from my brokenness. I knew it was difficult for her to see me groping with the past, but I assured her it was altogether necessary. I began to feel more and more free. The seventeen-year-old burden was lifted, and new life began! God allowed this seed to die, and He brought forth life.

The best mirror is an old friend. Traditional proverb

Maryjo was a friend who had weathered the storms of life with me. She bore with my fear of facing failure for many years. When I was finally ready to face that failure, she was there with open arms ready to forgive. She released me from my guilt and shame. Maryjo demonstrated for me that it was indeed finished. She became God's promise keeper to me, visibly showing me through her forgiveness just how completely God had forgiven me. She was the living, active body of my gracious Savior that day. That, my friend, is the power of lifegiving, enduring friendships.

Speaking words of encouragement

"A word aptly spoken is like apples of gold in settings of silver" (Proverbs 25:11). These are encouraging words, powerful words,

Simple Lifegiving . . . Dealing with Hurtful Words

When your friend says something that hurts you . . .

- Resist the temptation to rehearse the words.

- As the words replay in your mind, let them be a reminder to pray a blessing over your friend—return blessing for cursing (Luke 6:28).

- Write your friend a note telling her something kind that she said in the past that you appreciate.

- Call your friend and talk about something that you have in common that is pleasant and noncontroversial. Love covers a multitude of sins (1 Peter 4:8).

- Patiently allow the Holy Spirit to do His work.

- Guard your own mouth so that you do not unwittingly retaliate when you see your friend (Psalm 141:3).

lifegiving words. A wise and influential woman realizes that her words have the unique power to give hope where a heart is hopeless, peace in a place of turmoil, and confidence to the soul that is fearful.

As a child, did you know a woman with this extraordinary gift? A woman who spoke words of praise filled with promise? You could not wait to be in the presence of this woman. She had a key to your heart. Her words shaped your view of yourself, others, and the world in which you lived.

In contrast, you may also have known a death-dealing, life-zapping woman, maybe an unhappy aunt or neighbor. She always had a harsh word, a critical comment, and a never-ending list of complaints. You *friendships*

never wanted to be in her presence and would go to extremes to avoid her. Possibly the pain of her words can still be felt today. Memories like these prove once again the staying power of lifegiving and death-dealing words. They can affect us in lasting ways. Words can plant death and destruction, or they can bring forth life and encouragement. They build up or tear down. Lifegiving women know this. They know that their words can speak life into others, minimizing their shortcomings, maximizing their strengths, and encouraging them to live life more fully.

> Water and words are easy to pour but impossible to recover.
> Chinese proverb

True lifegiving friends see each other through the eyes of forgiveness and grace. Lifegivers know that what they focus on grows in importance to them. Because of this, they learn to bridle their critical tongues and negative thoughts. Scripture gives us much guidance in the area of our speech.

> For out of the overflow of the heart the mouth speaks. The good man brings good things out of the good stored up in him, and the evil man brings evil things out of the evil stored up in him. (Matthew 12:34–35)
>
> Do not let any unwholesome talk come out of your mouths, but only what is helpful for building others up according to their needs, that it may benefit those who listen. (Ephesians 4:29)

Do you find yourself focusing on the lack in others? Do you weigh their weaknesses against your strengths? When you speak, what flows from your heart to the ears of others? Our words really do reveal the

Abundant Lifegiving . . . Host a Birthday Luncheon!

- Plan a simple theme for your party, such as a summertime garden theme or a "something silver" gift theme.

- Send out snappy invitations or make calls. Pick a day that is good for your guest of honor. Build anticipation.

- Ask one or more friends to help with the food. For example, you may plan a salad luncheon and ask one friend to bring several kinds of breads, and ask another friend to bring the cake or dessert. Having help will make you feel less overwhelmed, and they can share in the fun of planning, too!

- Visit a local discount store, and purchase nice floral paper luncheon plates with matching napkins. Or, if you have nice dishes or china, use them! Dishes don't belong dusted in cupboards! They were meant to be used and enjoyed.

- Plan a simple menu.

- Put some small bowls of nuts and little candies in the middle of the table.

- After you eat lunch, as each gift is opened, ask the giver to share a lifegiving memory or encouragement with the birthday guest. Ask your guests to plan ahead to share a verse, quote, story, or what they most appreciate about this friend. These words will be keepsakes for a rainy day in the future! (Hey, it's a great thing to tape and listen to when life is feeling a bit dreary!)

friendships

attitude of our hearts. When we learn this truth, we can go to our Lord and ask Him to forgive our critical words and cleanse our selfish hearts. Then we can begin to see others the way Christ sees them, through the eyes of love and forgiveness. We are learning the art of minimizing shortcomings.

> You can make more friends in two months by becoming interested in other people than you can in two years by trying to get other people interested in you. Dale Carnegie

My friend Lynn has a wonderful ability to see my strengths and overlook my weaknesses. Her words of encouragement are like a healing balm that brings forth life in me. I vividly remember when Lynn moved into our Dallas neighborhood. We had just had a major flood in our home and had to move into a hotel for six weeks while repairs were being made. The first time I met Lynn, I had just come back to the house to begin cleaning. I was wearing yellow rubber gloves up to my armpits and not a drop of makeup, my dirty hair was thrown into a messy ponytail, and I was chasing my naked child who was running down the alley! Talk about a warm welcome to the neighborhood! None of this fazed Lynn. I think she learned to love me *because* of it. In fact, she jumped right in and made us the best-tasting tuna sandwiches for lunch.

When we maximize others' strengths, something powerful happens: We let go of the trap of comparison. We see, as lifegiving friends, that another's strength can be a rich well from which we draw. One lifegiving friend may have a beautiful, bold, and generous personality. Another woman might be intimidated by her and wonder if she could ever measure up to someone so strong and gifted. This is a deathblow to the relationship. But as we learn that the very strength in another's life is what causes us to grow, we become rich in an area we formerly knew nothing about. We see past external appearances to the potential within.

A real friend sticks closer than a brother. Proverbs 18:24 (NLT)

You too can have lifegiving friendships! If you already have strong female friendships, continue to pour life into each other and invest in the relationships you have. If you are longing for this kind of friendship, then resolve to meet new women and begin to build strong foundations of friendship. Maximize a new friend's strengths, appreciate her gifts and talents, receive strength from her, avoid the pitfall of comparison, and take delight in who she is. Everyone has weaknesses—including you and me. But as lifegiving women, we will not let these shortcomings keep us from the joy of friendship. Cultivating a garden of lifegiving friendship takes time and patience. To enjoy the fragrant blossoms of friendship, we not only enjoy the celebrations, but we also weather the storms of life together. It is time to plant! The sooner you sow your seed, the sooner you will enjoy the fragrance of your friendship garden.

chapter eight

Lifegiving through
Hospitality

hospitality

Here a dinner was

given in Jesus' honor.

Martha served.

John 12:2

Ever since I was a little girl, I have longed to make others feel welcome. Even now I have sweet memories of warm Sunday evenings helping my parents cook and prepare for the arrival of several couples for coffee after church. The excitement of someone new coming to our home was cause for great celebration. My mom, graced in her "good" white apron, would set a lovely table, cream china rimmed in simple silver.

The scents of rich, aromatic coffee brewing, meatballs frying, and buns baking filled the small kitchen of our home. I remember pulling up a kitchen stool and watching as my mother poured rich, heavy cream into an old peach can and hand-whipped it into artistic peaks. (Of course, I was secretly hoping to lick the beater!) This mountain of whipped cream topped off the fresh apple pie she had baked the day before. Billows of steam from a glazed ham wafted though the house, announcing that guests were indeed on their way. I always loved helping and simply cherished the energy and excitement that hospitality brought to our home.

Although my skill in hospitality has grown a bit in the last thirty years, the foundational elements were laid down in me by the hand of my first mentor, my gracious mother. This is the wonderful heritage a lifegiving woman gives her children.

Good food, delicious smells, the promise of a shared meal, words and actions that convey encouragement—is this all there is to hospitality? Does hospitality require great culinary skill, creativity, and an outgoing personality? These are assets, but, sister, these are not requirements in showing hospitality. Simply put, by a dear friend who has practiced hospitality faithfully for over forty years, Phyllis Stanley says, *"Hospitality is a message we give people about their value."* And that is what my mom taught me, not in word but in deed.

Then I grew up and moved away from my mother's hearth and

home to begin my own life of hospitality. This, my friend, has been a very insightful journey. Throughout this voyage I was learning to be the lifegiving, hospitable woman God created me to be. Though at times this journey has seemed challenging, nothing has brought more joy to our family than inviting guests to our home.

The life without festival is a long road without an inn. Democritus of Abdera

---

The journey has had a few sharp twists and turns along the way. Shortly after Butch and I were married, I was determined to be the ultimate hospitable wife. My mom seemed to have it down to a science, and I was determined to master the craft as well. (Oh, did I have much to learn!) I did all the homework. I read every book on entertaining I could find. I embraced all the flashy, impressive methods and practiced, practiced, practiced. I became a taskmaster in the realm of entertaining. I always had a diligent plan, an action-packed meal, and music and candles that made my house look like something out of a romantic Victorian novel. This was serious! Nobody could mess up my cooking schedule, my picture-perfect house, or my napkins, which were folded in some unique, foreign bird design. The food must look like a magazine cover, the children like they just stepped out of a Ralph Lauren ad, and the house like it was straight from *Architectural Digest*.

The problem was that my rigid idea of the perfect evening of entertaining created, well, a bit of an uptight atmosphere. I was not fostering much in the way of spontaneous fun or heartfelt comfort. I made Martha from the Gospels look like a lightweight!

Speaking of Martha from the Gospels, don't you think she has gotten a pretty bad rap? A woman who would chop olives, dice figs, and knead bread while the others just sat around chatting . . . well, I mean, really! Who where these people anyway?

Oh?

Christ, the Son of the living God?

Hmmmm . . .

So, what did she say to Him? Let's look and see.

> As Jesus and his disciples were on their way, he came to a village where a woman named Martha opened her home to him. She had a sister called Mary, who sat at the Lord's feet listening to what he said. But Martha was distracted by all the preparations that had to be made. She came to him and asked, "Lord, don't you care that my sister has left me to do the work by myself? Tell her to help me!" (Luke 10:38–40)

Do you remember how He responded?

> "Martha, Martha," the Lord answered, "you are worried and upset about many things, but only one thing is needed. Mary has chosen what is better, and it will not be taken away from her." (Luke 10:41–42)

Every time I read these verses, I realize how easily I could have been Miss Martha. I understand her frustration and her focus. I want to rise to defend this lifegiver. Oh yes, she was a lifegiver!

See, what Martha was doing was not bad. In fact, everyone would have missed her delicious homemade fig pie right around dinner time. What Jesus was really telling Martha was a gentle reminder, something like this: "Martha, what you are doing is good, and I know you think it is best. But Mary is choosing what is better. You see, I will only be in your home a few hours, and then I will be on My way. My desire is to be *with* you, to connect *with* you, and for you to understand how I long to *touch your heart*. Let's just have tea and day-old figs. I love fig pie, but I love time *with* you more."

As Martha did, so I too had missed the whole point of bringing friends and family into our home. And I had missed it big. The focus was all about *me: my* hard work, *my* tasks, *my* elaborate yet lifeless meals, *my* perfect presentation. And when things got messed up (which they always did), I became angry and resentful and huffed really, really loud. I started barking out orders, making sure everyone knew that I had sacrificed all day so that they could have a "wonderful time together."

To be a good host, don't pretend to be other than you are. Emily Post

---

By the time our guests left, I was filled with disappointment and frustration. Something or someone had to change. Of course, my first thought was that it was "something" that needed to go. *If my husband would help me more, if the kids would cooperate with my plan and act a bit more accommodating, maybe I could be the lifegiving hospitality queen I long to be.* Sadly enough, none of these well-crafted excuses or the many others I rehearsed in my head hit the heart of the issue.

Yes, it was a heart issue. I needed to drastically change my understanding of what hospitality was. The someone that needed to change was me, and this change needed to come from the *inside out*.

What I did not understand is that *true hospitality begins with the right mind-set, a way of thinking about the well-being and happiness of others*. Hospitality involves giving generously and treating our guests genuinely and with consideration of who they are. This approach to hospitality creates an atmosphere of warmth and acceptance.

Romans 12:13 admonishes us, "Share with God's people who are in need. Practice hospitality." Hospitality is an opportunity to practice loving others. We practice so that we become better and more Christlike with each encounter. When we practice, we become more confident with our skills and gifts.

Interestingly enough, Jesus also tells His disciples to love strangers and even enemies. And what is an enemy? Is it someone who has a vehement hatred for us and wants to kill us? That may be true, but it is not the norm. Actually, an enemy can be defined as anyone who does not have our interests at heart, who does not care for our needs, who is absorbed with his or her own concerns with no consideration for ours. Think of it. We are asked by God to love those who are not going to reciprocate our love, and we may need to show that love through hospitality. The Lord says,

> If you love those who love you, what credit is that to you? Even "sinners" love those who love them. And if you do good to those who are good to you, what credit is that to you? Even "sinners" do that. And if you lend to those from whom you expect repayment, what credit is that to you? Even "sinners" lend to "sinners," expecting to be repaid in full. But love your enemies, do good to them, and lend to them without expecting to get anything back. Then your reward will be great, and you will be sons of the Most High, because he is kind to the ungrateful and wicked. Be merciful, just as your Father is merciful. (Luke 6:32–36)

Remember what we studied about the Secret Life of the Lifegiver? When we give unto the Lord, giving when we cannot be repaid, that puts our reward in a place where moth and rust do not decay. That gets God's attention.

The most mystifying verse on the subject of hospitality is Hebrews 13:2, which urges us, "Do not forget to entertain strangers, for by so doing some people have entertained angels without knowing it." Imagine it! We may someday be giving the loving comfort of a meal or even a cup of cold water to an angel without knowing it. I cannot possibly explain this concept to you, but this I know.

Several years ago while I was flying for the airlines, I had the most unusual encounter. I was on a layover in Portland, Oregon, using my limited layover time to shop in the downtown area. It was a cold afternoon, overcast and a bit depressing. I was running from store to store to escape the drizzling rain and to try to put a dent in my Christmas shopping.

> Small things done in great love bring great joy. Mother Teresa

The day sped by as normal; hours of power shopping and plenty of packages offered proof to my success. As I was entering one last store before heading back to my hotel, I saw a disheveled, old, homeless man. He sat quietly by the front doors, on a large cardboard box, missing both legs, and clearly in need of help. I was in a hurry to finish my shopping, and I quickly breezed through the front door. As I passed him, I glanced in his direction, trying to hide my horror.

We made eye contact, and I was clearly uncomfortable. I half-smiled at him and pushed my way quickly through the doors. Though a bit startled by his desperate appearance, I quickly moved on to accomplish my "To Do" list. (Oh, here comes Martha again!) As I was bustling through the store, the Lord spoke to me. "Tammy, I want you to push past what you are comfortable with, push past what you understand and what you can control, and simply give that man money for lunch. Oh yes, and tell him I love and care for him deeply."

Not this again. *Okay, Lord, but what if he just spends the money on alcohol or drugs?* (Ever heard that excuse?) *What will people think of me stooping down to speak with him, handing this very dirty, downright scary-looking man anything? Really, God, does this bring You joy?*

I must have gone up and down the escalator five times (really!), but I just could not shake it. So I headed over to the door. As I pushed through the circular glass, I instantly made eye contact with him. It was as if he knew I would return. "Hi, my name is Tammy, and I just wanted to give you some money for lunch." I handed him a ten-dollar bill. "I also wanted you to know God told me to tell you He loves and cares about you."

Time endures, but cannot fade the memories that love made. Anonymous

He reached up to take the money and said, "I saw you go into the store. God told me you would be the one to help me today. I waited for the moment you would come back." He continued to stare at me with piercing eyes. "But what you must know is this was a gift for you, from the loving hand of God. For He tests and rewards all acts done in His name." I nervously smiled and turned toward the road. *I kept thinking about what he had said and how he had said it.* It felt so unreal. As I stepped toward the busy street, only feet from where this man was huddled, I turned to look at him one more time. He was gone. There was simply no trace of the man. I was so shaken I could hardly walk. I went up and down the street looking for him. It would have been impossible for him to walk away and highly improbable for him to be carried away. I was right there. Only a moment had passed and he was gone. Even as I remember this, I am crying at the sweetness of Jesus. Oh yes, I believe in angels.

To show hospitality on any level is to show love, and love is the crowning virtue of the lifegiving woman. There are countless ways to show hospitality. Giving ten dollars to a man on the street is an unusual venue of loving hospitality. Perhaps you may express hospitality by making your home available for a Bible study or a church gathering or by simply seeing to it that a neighborhood child feels loved and welcomed in your home. It may be providing a cold drink or a hot meal for someone who needs encouragement. Sometimes hospitality is a spur-of-the-moment thing—inviting a neighbor in for coffee or baking store-bought cookie dough with a single mom and her children. At other times, hospitality requires planning, such as an elegant meal for twenty. Loving hospitality has many faces and reflections.

True hospitality sends the message to our guests that they are important, that we thought about them, that we planned for their presence in our home. In fact, giving them a sense of their value is why we do what we do! Hospitality speaks volumes to others about our genuine love for them and reminds them that they are significant to us.

Food tastes better when there is beauty to behold. Terry Willits

---

Okay, now let's look back to Martha. Because I identified with her so strongly, I was determined to find out if she made any progress in her hospitality. So I read everything I could about the life and times of Martha. Did you know that in the Gospel of John, we find Martha serving again? She served another meal to the Lord. Read the account with me.

> Six days before the Passover, Jesus arrived at
> Bethany, where Lazarus lived, whom Jesus had
> raised from the dead. Here a dinner was given in

Jesus' honor. **Martha served,** while Lazarus was among those reclining at the table with him. (John 12:1–2, emphasis mine)

Interesting, isn't it? What was the difference this time? I see it this way. The first time around, "serving others" *had* Martha. The focus was on her and her agenda. Thus the Lord disciplined her in love. He helped her to refocus on what was truly "the best thing." In round two, she understood the best thing. Yet she still served a meal to the Lord. I think she had learned the beauty and freedom in hospitality. *The first time the demands gripped her; the second time she realized the tasks were a tool to express love.*

Maybe you are a Martha type, troubled by many things, overburdened by a need to create a perfect environment anytime a guest walks through your door. If so, learn with me a simple way to create beauty, comfort, and love through your hospitality.

Dining is and always was a great artistic opportunity. Frank Lloyd Wright

Or you may be so like Mary that serving dinner or any other meal to guests is never associated with your name. Perhaps you are just apprehensive about serving others in your home or you doubt that you are an acceptable cook or hostess. Actually, this is the plight of many women. The issue is not overdoing, like Martha, but not doing much at all. If this is you, dear sister, I have many fun and easy ideas for you! I have included a few simple recipes to get you started in your practice of hospitality. As you grow in lifegiving hospitality, your guests will not only be fed in body; they will also be nourished in soul. This is the heart of lifegiving hospitality.

Imagine approaching the door of a friend's home. Your heart is filled with anticipation. For one thing, you know you do not have to cook tonight. (Ya gotta love that!) Everyone knows a meal tastes so much better when someone else makes it. You have looked forward to this night all day. And even decided to put on something beautiful just to feel special. As you reach for the doorbell, your mood is light. You are ready to relax, sit back, and enjoy.

How are you so sure that these qualities of pleasure will characterize the evening? Because you know and trust your friend's feelings toward you. You know her loving ways, her thoughtfulness, and her care for her guests. She is a lifegiving woman, and she has in mind the happiness and comfort of those who visit her home as she prepares a place for them. Is she wealthy, able to spare no expense on foods and table settings? Probably not. But she is lavish in love and rich in kindness.

As the door opens, you are welcomed with open arms. You step across the threshold and see that she has indeed prepared a place for you. A blanket of cozy comfort seems to wrap around you as you are ushered to the carefully laid table, lit with candlelight and fragrant with fresh flowers. Somehow this mirrors that abundant life way back in the garden.

Chances are that one of the reasons you so anticipated dinner at the home of your good friend is that you knew she would prepare a special place for you. If you had been to her home for dinner in the past only to find pandemonium and a box of macaroni next to a boiling pot of water, you may not have had such a sense of anticipation. Of course, we all love being with our friends for drop-in visits and actually feel better when we walk in and find things a little bit crazy. We are happy to see that our friend has a real life too! I always tell people that they will like me better when they see what my life really looks like (fifteen loads of laundry tall and a pantry door that MUST stay shut!).

But when we are invited to a lifegiving friend's house for dinner, we know that all things will have been made ready. We know that when we go there, we will receive life and that when we leave there, we will take that life home with us. We will drink from the well in that home and find refreshment. Somehow we know that all the preparations will have been made, that the conversation will be uplifting, the food will be familiar and yet special, and that we will leave feeling the comfort of love and lifegiving.

So how can you and I prepare such a place for our guests? We long to give others a message about their value by having them in our homes, yet we often fear the weight of entertaining and the insecurities about whether or not we will burn dinner. We wonder if the kids will act crazy. Worse yet, we wonder if our guests will actually enjoy our company.

Is successful hospitality just a "happy accident"? I think not! Intentional preparation, thinking through what needs to be accomplished before our guests arrive, and doing those things properly in advance is what will ensure a relaxing experience.

When I am frazzled and overburdened by too many things to be done at the last minute—like Martha was in Luke 10—I am not able to wind down and be relaxed by the time the doorbell rings. Even before we get into specific preparations, here are a few basic ideas to keep in mind.

First of all, plan for simplicity. We do not need elaborate décor, expensive table settings, and gourmet recipes to prepare a fabulous dinner or to have a few friends over for appetizers or dessert. Simple things can be beautiful and tasty.

Use fresh flowers if at all possible when setting your table, but in summertime, pick them from your garden instead of the florist. Even humble flowers like fresh-cut geraniums or pansies placed down the center of the table in a series of small vases make the setting seem special to your guests.

Bake an easy cake instead of buying one. Buy good ice cream. It may be vanilla or another basic flavor, but premium ice cream, which only costs a few dollars more, makes the dessert seem richer. Simple touches like that make the whole meal seem special.

Next, serve the predictable. Who doesn't like a BLT sandwich? You may think this is the last thing you should consider serving a friend for lunch. Yet we all like to eat what is familiar. The familiar brings comfort. So, serve up BLT sandwiches for lunch, but use the best mayonnaise, the freshest bread, the juiciest tomatoes, and the crispest lettuce, and you will have one of the best, yet most familiar, lunches imaginable!

Whatever you would do, begin it. Boldness has courage, genius and magic in it. Goethe

---

I like to serve dishes I have made over and over again. This guarantees confidence. If you have found one group of company loves one of your recipes, then you can be confident that the next group will love it just as much. Stick with a good repertoire of solid recipes and always use fresh, fresh, fresh ingredients.

Finally, plan for your guests' happiness. Take loving responsibility for the happiness of your guests for the few hours they will be in your home. *Truly welcome them!* Greet them at the door with open arms and warm words. Being delighted that they are in your home is the true spirit of hospitality, and that joy is contagious.

Think of hospitality—having people in your home for a short time—as a way of easing the trouble of their day. It is a way of capturing time and wrapping it up in a lovely package with a beautiful bow to be unwrapped by each guest as they sit with you. Even if you burn dinner (Personal confession: One time I burned something so badly it took a fire extinguisher to get it out!) or catch the centerpiece on fire (Yes, I have done this too!), you have lovingly made all things ready. You have invited life's weary travelers to come and sup for a while, to forget their troubles and enjoy the comfort of lifegiving friendship. It is a foretaste of heaven right here on earth. Heaven in my own kitchen.

Recently I had my dear neighbor, a practicing Mormon, over for lunch to celebrate her birthday. (Okay, so it was six months late.) I served simple tea sandwiches, fruit, and, of course, a relish dish (my Minnesota upbringing shining through!). We chatted about all kinds of things—kids, work, and the love of God. As we were sharing, my friend's eyes misted with tears. She painfully told me her husband claimed he did not love her anymore, and she felt her heart would break. While sipping tea and eating egg salad sandwiches, God gave me a beautiful opportunity to lead her to a personal relationship with Jesus Christ.

Dream-furniture is the only kind on which you never stub your toes or bang your knee. C. S. Lewis

---

Why did this happen then? Well, of course the Lord was wooing her. He loved her and desired a relationship with her. But what I find so interesting is the setting—in my family room, eating egg salad sandwiches and relishes. Somehow it felt warm and safe. Gene Barron said, "The world will not care what we know until they know that we care." She had somehow felt a sense of comfort. She knew I cared.

This is the simple beauty and great reward of hospitality. Was it elaborate? Definitely not. Was it difficult? Not at all. It just took moments to prepare my home and heart, and a lifegiving memory was born.

Perhaps you are wondering how you can possibly provide this type of experience in your six-hundred-square-foot apartment. Or you may live in a six-thousand-square-foot, professionally decorated home and have a career that barely allows time to boil water for tea, let alone plan a dinner party! All life circumstances are fraught with constraints and limitations. You must lift your sights to see the possibilities.

Regardless of your situation, look for ways to give. You, living in the small apartment—pull two chairs together next to a table, make a tray of appetizers, light a candle, put a few simple flowers in a vase, and hand a refreshing drink of pear juice and sparkling water to your friend as she walks through the door. (Put a couple of frozen green grapes in—it looks fabulous!)

When Butch and I were first married, we returned from our wedding to share our nine-hundred-square-foot apartment with a mom and her two children. They lived with us for several months until they were able to find a place of their own. As I look back on that time I remember it with fondness. Oh yes, there were interesting moments when one bathroom was just not enough! But this woman became a real mentor to me and helped shape me. I have always been blessed when God has given me a chance to share my home with someone in need, no matter the size of my house.

Perhaps you, dear sister, live in the big house and have no time but plenty of resources. Invite three or five or seven friends for dinner and cater the meal. Spend a few minutes each evening before the event setting up a lovely table. Live a little! And for the rest of you in between, realize you *can* do it! We all can create a happy, lovely place for our guests. Remember, true hospitality is giving someone a message about his or her value. It is a heart issue, not a size issue.

Planning ahead

Success is the result of persistence, patience, planning, and personal initiative. Planning is one of the greatest elements to successful, confident hospitality. Plan for your sake and for your guests' overall comfort. Be ready before they arrive. If you are well-prepared, you will have the opportunity to be *with* your guests, not just stuck in the kitchen serving them. This is a practical key to enjoying others in your home. Everything else—the menu, the decorations, and the table settings—comes *after* you have embraced the most important element . . . your guests.

There are five key elements in preparing for successful hospitality. Plan well in these areas, and you will be assured a wonderful experience. The five key things we need to put in order are our hearts, our home, our family, the meal, and the delicious doggy bag.

Our Hearts

First, we get our hearts ready. In the chapter on the Secret Life of the Lifegiver, we discussed the many facets of heart preparation. We identified the significant difference between being a do-gooder and a lifegiver. As we seek to abide in Christ, as we die to our self-life and allow His life to be made manifest in what we do and say, as we cultivate a lifegiving garden and allow the dead things in our lives to be redeemed by the Lord and turned into lifegiving potential, then we find our hearts are full to overflowing. Then our hearts are ready to give.

Our Home

Next, we prepare our homes. This part does include a "To Do" list. Clean the bathroom, put out fresh flowers, sweep the floor, set the table, set out bowls of nuts, decide what lights to turn on and where to place the candles, etc. Yet the lifegiving woman is doing more than setting the silverware according to Emily Post; she is creating *a tone, a mood*. She has this mood in mind as she prepares her home. (You do not have to clean all the bedrooms every time you entertain. My rule is that no one goes upstairs—ever!) This brought a newfound freedom to having people in my home . . . with four very real, very messy children! All these components working together create a warm, comfortable ambiance. They are an unwritten welcome sign for your guests.

Beauty draws you in but comfort keeps you there. Terry Willits

---

When I prepare, I always begin with my table setting. Plan something that you know will give them pleasure, not one that will simply impress. Set the table a day or two before your guests arrive. I have a friend who sets her table a few days ahead so she can enjoy the beauty and anticipate the event. Having your table ready reduces your stress when the day arrives, and it will also be a source of excitement for you and your family. Anticipation is half the fun.

Try to include flowers, always freshly cut in a vase. Make sure your beautiful centerpiece is not too high. Your guests will want to be able to see over it and talk freely with others around the table. Remember that fresh flowers bring so much life. Although I am not a fan of silk flowers, if they are used creatively, they can work. If you use silk flowers, lay them down the center of the table or wrap them around the base of a candlestick.

Use candles! The warm glow of candlelight creates a comfortable feeling. Etiquette books suggest no candlelight before 4 P.M. Why wait? Even a daytime luncheon with a friend is warmed by the flicker of flames in small votives scattered down the table. My kids laugh at all the candles around our house, but the beauty of it has caught on with them. As soon as it gets a bit dim in the house, my girls (and Sam too) start lighting every candle they see. They know I love it, and it speaks peace to them, too.

I have found that some of the best resources for creating a lovely table setting are magazines and entertaining books. *Copy, copy, copy!* If I can see a picture or watch it being created, I can do it—but don't ask me to start from scratch. Don't just copy; copy cheap by improvising. Check your local discount department store that sells items that may have once been in major department stores, and you will be amazed at what you can find. Never think, *I could never do that!* Just look twice, and you will find the bargains, the cheaper version of the table linens, the dishes on sale at your favorite store. You do not have to buy a full five-piece service for ten or twelve when you want some new dinner plates. Just buy eight dinner plates. Or what if you need twelve settings and only have eight? Feel free to mix and match plates and patterns. I do it all the time. Find a color theme and add different plates and cups. Girl, this is very chic!

Our Family

You may or may not plan to include your children. (Believe it or not, this can actually be done successfully.) Before your guests arrive, sit down with your children or grandchildren and give them a few tips on how to act when your guests are present, and tell them your expectations of them personally. However, in spite of these little "pep talks," be prepared for the unpredictable!

Several years ago, Butch called and said he was bringing home three clients for a quick dinner. (Quick for whom?) This was serious cause for panic. *What am I going to make?* Boxes of macaroni and cheese and creamy peanut butter filled the cupboard. *What does my house look like?* Alas, I painfully knew. *What will I do with the four children ages eight and way, way under?* Hide them far, far away?

As dinnertime approached and the company was on their merry way (not company—clients!), I had a little talk with the children. "Okay, dear ones, listen up. Dad is bringing home some very important people. These people are called *clients*. Simply put, they pay for your food and lodging. If you want to live a long and prosperous life, go to college, and get married, you need to be on your best, most magnificent and angelic behavior. Got it?"

They all looked at me with little faces that said, "Oh goodness, Mom, of course. Our goal in life is to make you look like you have everything under control. Nothing could be our greater joy." Everyone but Mikia, that is.

Mikia is my humbling factor. Do you have one of those in your family? If you do, you clearly understand why I was a bit concerned when she broke out in a big smile and said, "Whatever you say, Mama dearest!" and skipped glibly out of the kitchen. For a very precocious four-year-old, this meant trouble.

A good laugh is sunshine in a house. William Makepeace Thackeray

---

Before I go any further, let me give you the frightening rundown of the company for the evening. One gentleman—let's call him Bob—had never been married, let alone graced a dinner table with four children under the age of eight. His conversations were seasoned with comments such as, "Did you know that [names elegant French wine] has the most surpassingly lovely nose?" to "Did you hear about the great deal he got on his breathtakingly beautiful Italian villa?" Needless to say, it was a totally different world than mine.

Another woman—let's call her Sue—had just had her first baby. She was a very efficient, organized, clearly undaunted new mother. She had one of those smiles that said, "Well, my children will never do that! Perhaps you need to read the newest book on . . ." She was indeed the most well-read "expert" on raising kids I had ever met.

Then there was another gentleman—let's call him George. George was a nice guy, but he had two grown children who were independent and painfully well-mannered. He could not quite remember when the kids were small, but he was sure that they once were.

So this rather unique group of individuals sat down at my kitchen table for a meal of Apple Chicken and veggies with four small (but not to be underestimated) Maltby offspring. Yet all seemed to be going well. The children were right in line with my orders, saying please and thank you at the right times. The *image* seemed to be well within reach.

Then came the painstaking, out-of-control, child-inspired avalanche. "Mommy," said that blue-eyed, blond-haired, innocent four-year-old (She was dangerous!), "May I please be excused to use the bathroom?"

Reluctantly I allowed Mikia to meander down the hall to the bathroom. She slipped off the bench that held the four children, and with a magnificent smile, she merrily skipped down the hall. She was going to have a serious encounter with the potty.

The adult conversation continued and was seasoned with "Yes," "Oh, how interesting," "Well, I simply never knew that." Trying earnestly to be an interested and hospitable wife, I chatted with them about many and varied things. Moments later, in the midst of a discussion of the national deficit and the need for more inner-city missions, we heard Mikia quite loudly from down the hall.

"UMMMMM! Oh my goodness, here it comes, the big daddy one! . . . Ooh, look, the momma is on her way. . . . and oh, it's four little baby ones! Oh Mama, it's so cute! Maaaamaaaa!!! Come here and see this!"

At first I wanted to die, and then I was afraid I wouldn't. Everyone stopped talking. Everyone was listening. We were captive to Mikia's play-by-play creation of a family of bowel movements.

The other children were on the floor laughing, my dear private husband Butch looked a unique shade of pale green, and our guests appeared to all have a case of medical shock. And if that were not bad enough, Mikia came bottom first into the kitchen to see if anyone would help her wipe her little derrière! Alas, one must always be prepared for the unexpected when children are involved.

The Meal

Remember, hospitality is not about perfection; it is about comfort. As you begin to think about your meal, try to plan food that you know your guests will be fond of and find tasty, not necessarily recipes that show off your culinary skill. If your friend has a Middle Eastern background, whip up a batch of humus dip with pita triangles for an appetizer. Or if your friend is Hispanic, find the best tamales in the city and incorporate them into the meal. If you know your guests' tastes, then find a simple way to please them with predictable and familiar fare. That will communicate comfort to them.

APPETIZERS, ANYONE?

Presenting hors d'oeuvres in a visually alluring way is as important as the enticing and delicious flavors they promise. All this takes is a bit of creativity on your part. Look around your home for pieces that are interesting. Oddly shaped baskets, large wooden platters, even a nice wood chopping block, tall ceramic or glass jars, square or round pedestal cake stands stacked on one another, colored tile pieces, or a marble cutting board—the list is really endless. One of the most frequent compliments I receive while entertaining is, "Wow, I never thought of using that!"

Another tip in presenting beautiful hors d'oeuvres is to incorporate color and interest in choosing your tray lining. You can use different salad greens. My favorite garnish is the banana leaf. Not only is it unique, but it also holds up well throughout the evening. I also love to use clumps of natural herbs, edible flowers (such as pansies), baby-sized fruits (such as kumquats), large cinnamon sticks tied together, oversized chunks of rock salt, and nuts in a variety of shapes and colors.

The Baked Brie recipe is a staple recipe that has been used in my kitchen for years. When I make my Baked Brie and fill it with cranberry chutney, I add a bit of visual interest by lining my platter with banana leaves surrounded by fresh cranberries, bright orange kumquats, and mint leaves. It tastes grand and looks impressive, too. I often modify ingredients to give it a new twist. Just by changing the jams or by adding fresh seasonings (i.e., parsley and mint), I give it a new and inviting twist.

Baked Brie

Nothing satisfies like a warm, creamy cheese. This recipe is so easy that you can make it in three minutes. And the presentation is unreal! Buy extra Brie cheese rounds and puff pastry sheets and keep them in your freezer. You will always have a wonderful hors d'oeuvre to serve at a moment's notice.

1 14-ounce round Brie
1 package puffed pastry sheets (found in the section of the freezer where you find pie crusts)
Any variety of jams, chutneys (apricot is my personal favorite), dried fruits, and nuts

Remove one sheet of the frozen puff pastry. Let it come to

room temperature (or microwave on defrost for 2 minutes). Cut Brie in half lengthwise. Place one slice of the Brie (creamy side up) in the center of the unfolded puff pastry sheet. Add approximately 1/3 cup of whatever filling you choose. Place other half of Brie (creamy side down) on top of fruit mixture.

Carefully wrap the puff pastry upward around the Brie. Starting with the corners of the pastry, fold up in a circle fashion around the Brie, gathering the ends in the center of the Brie. Place on foil-lined and sprayed cookie sheet, seam side down. Brush with egg.

Bake at 375° for 15 to 20 minutes, until golden brown. Let stand 5 minutes before cutting.

APPLE, BRIE, AND PROSCIUTTO BRUSCHETTA

This has become my new personal favorite. You can change the meat to peppered turkey and the fruit to a soft pear. But always use the fresh rosemary—it makes it wonderful.

1, 4-1/2-ounce round Brie cheese (or other white, soft cheese)
16, 1/4-inch thick slices French bread baguette
1 Tablespoon melted butter or olive oil
4 ounces thinly sliced prosciutto, cut in 2-inch pieces
1 medium Fuji or Granny Smith apple, cut into 16 slices
3 teaspoons finely snipped fresh rosemary (or as much as desired)

Cut chilled Brie into eight wedges crosswise.

Place bread slices on a baking sheet. Broil about 6 inches from heat for 1 to 2 minutes or until lightly toasted. Turn slices; brush topsides lightly with melted butter. Broil 1 to 2 minutes more or until lightly toasted. Remove from oven.

Divide prosciutto, apple, and Brie among toasted bread. Sprinkle with rosemary. Broil 2 minutes more or until cheese begins to soften. Serve warm. Makes 16 servings.

Dessert!

When you want to bake something easy that looks like you were in the kitchen all day, try the Maltby Cake. I have made this cake for more than ten years. At last count, I have made over five hundred of these glorious cakes! Teachers get them for just being my kids' teachers, friends for birthday parties, and my kids for celebration days. I have shared this cake with neighbors for just moving into the neighborhood. You will have so much fun presenting this cake to your guests. And the best part is that this is made from a boxed cake mix!

The Maltby Cake

1 box vanilla cake mix (any kind with pudding in it)
1 small chocolate instant pudding mix
1 small vanilla instant pudding mix
4 eggs (5 for high altitude)
1-1/2 cups water
1/2 cup vegetable oil
1 cup chocolate chips (dark or bittersweet)
1 cup chopped nuts (if desired)
1/2 cup flour (if high altitude)
1 pint whipping cream
chocolate-dipped strawberries

Mix first nine ingredients lightly by hand 50 strokes or by mixer 20 seconds. (There will be some mix that has not blended well.) Pour into 2 round cake pans (8 or 9 inch), greased well and floured if necessary. Bake at 350° for approximately 40 minutes. Remove cakes, place on cooling rack, and cool to room temperature. Beat whipping cream till very firm. Add powdered sugar and vanilla to taste.

Put fern greens on cake plate. Add one of the cakes on top. Frost with whipped cream. Add next layer of cake and frost whole cake with the remaining whipped cream. Top with chocolate-dipped strawberries. Add remaining strawberries around the edges of the cake. Put in refrigerator and let chill.

Tip: If you desire to make a white cake, use only vanilla puddings and white chocolate chips.

DINNER IS SERVED!

Now you are ready to host dinner. On the following pages, you will find tried-and-true meals. They taste wonderful and are simple to prepare. After you have arranged any of these meals once, you know you can do it, again and again and again. You do not have to change your menu every time you have people over for dinner. If you have a busy lifestyle and have two dinners you need to host a few days apart or even one right after the other, just make twice as much and serve it both nights. It will be just as good both times. Or you can vary one part of the menu if you cannot stomach a total repeat.

Many good meals begin with or are accompanied by a fresh salad. The American public is obsessed with bags of prewashed and cut lettuces. What a time saver! Now we have no excuse not to offer salad at every meal.

MANDARIN ORANGE VINAIGRETTE SALAD

When making this salad, I always use organic field greens. They provide beautiful variety in color and tastes.

1 bag of prewashed and chopped lettuce or field greens
1 large can of mandarin oranges, drained
1 cup freshly grated Parmesan cheese
4 small green onions chopped finely
1 small bag of pre-shredded and washed carrots
Wish-Bone Italian Dressing

Place first five ingredients in a large bowl. Lightly toss in dressing. Serve with prepackaged breadsticks or fresh bagel chips.

CRANBERRY PINEAPPLE CHICKEN

This is downright yummy comfort food. Have the recipe close by. Your guests will beg for it!

3/4 cup all-purpose flour
1/2 teaspoon salt
1/2 teaspoon pepper
6 large boneless skinless chicken breasts cut in half
1/4 cup butter
2 Tablespoons olive oil
2 medium onions chopped
2 cups frozen cranberries
1 can crushed pineapple with liquid (2 large Granny Smith apples cut into thick slices may be used instead)
1 cup water
1 cup packed brown sugar
2 Tablespoons red wine vinegar
1 cup cooking or red wine
1/2 teaspoon nutmeg
1/2 teaspoon cinnamon

In a large plastic bag, combine flour, salt, and pepper. Put chicken in bag and shake two at a time. In a large skillet, melt better and oil. Add onion; cook until clear and tender. Remove from skillet. Add chicken until browned on both sides, about 10 minutes. Remove chicken and set aside.

In the same skillet, combine the onions, cranberries, pineapple, water, brown sugar, vinegar, red cooking wine, nutmeg, and cinnamon. Bring to boil and simmer for 20 minutes.

To assemble, layer half of the fruit mixture in bottom of a 9 x 13 casserole dish. Add chicken and cover with remaining fruit. Cover dish with foil. Bake covered at 375° for 50 minutes.

Remove foil and bake for 15 more minutes until mixture thickens. (Add a little water if mixture becomes too thick.)

hospitality

Transfer chicken to serving platter, cover with fruit, and garnish with fresh parsley.

Spring Beef

This is one of Tamra's favorite, easy-to-make dishes.

4 beef filets, cut 1 inch thick (or 2 pounds of less expensive steak)
Marinade:
1/2 cup soy sauce or Tamari soy
1/2 cup red cooking wine
1/4 cup olive oil
4 Tablespoons Worcestershire sauce
4 garlic cloves, crushed
Fresh ground pepper to taste

Prepare marinade in a 9 x 13 glass baking dish. Gently stir to mix ingredients. Place steaks in marinade. Turn immediately. Cover with plastic wrap and let sit at room temperature for 30 to 40 minutes (or let sit in refrigerator for up to 2 hours and bring to room temperature before grilling for best flavor). Grill or broil to taste.

Thai Chicken Wraps

This is my kids' all-time favorite meal. If your guests include children, this is a sure-fire winner.

6, 8- to 10-inch plain red (and/or green) flour tortillas
3/4 pound boneless, skinless chicken breast strips for stir-frying
1/2 teaspoon garlic salt
1/4 to 1/2 teaspoon pepper
1 Tablespoon cooking oil
4 cups packaged shredded broccoli (broccoli slaw mix)
1 medium red onion, cut into thin wedges
1 teaspoon grated fresh ginger

Wrap tortillas in paper towels. Microwave on high power for 30 seconds to soften. (Or wrap tortillas in foil and heat at 350° for 10 minutes.)

In a small bowl combine garlic salt and pepper. Add chicken; toss to coat evenly. In a large skillet, cook and stir seasoned chicken in hot oil over medium-high heat for 2 to 3 minutes or until no longer pink. Remove from skillet; keep warm. Add broccoli, onion, and ginger to skillet. Cook and stir for 2 to 3 minutes or until vegetables are crisp-tender.

To assemble, spread each tortilla with about 1 Tablespoon Peanut Sauce. Top with chicken strips and vegetable mixture. Roll up each tortilla, securing with a toothpick. Serve immediately with remaining sauce. Makes 6 servings.

PEANUT SAUCE:

- 1/4 cup sugar
- 1/4 cup creamy peanut butter
- 3 Tablespoons soy sauce
- 3 Tablespoons water
- 2 Tablespoons cooking oil
- 1 teaspoon bottled minced garlic

In a small saucepan, combine sugar, peanut butter, soy sauce, water, cooking oil, and bottled minced garlic. Heat until sugar is dissolved, stirring frequently. Makes about 2/3 cup.

CARDAMOM CARROTS

This delicious carrot side dish can be made ahead of time (up to three days) and stored in a Ziploc bag. When it is time to heat, microwave on high until steamy, then drop contents into bowl. Throw out bag—no mess or cleanup the night of your dinner.

- 1-1/2 pounds baby carrots
- 3/4 teaspoon ground cardamom (a bit pricey but worth it!)
- 1/2 teaspoon pepper

hospitality

1/4 teaspoon salt
2 Tablespoons chopped fresh parsley
1/4 cup honey
1 Tablespoon cornstarch
1/3 cup dry vermouth (dry white cooking wine)
1/2 cup butter
2 teaspoons grated lemon rind
1/4 cup lemon juice
1/4 cup orange juice

Cook carrots in small amount of boiling water for 7 to 8 minutes or until crisp-tender. Drain and plunge into cold water. (This is very important.) Set aside.

Combine cornstarch and vermouth (or cooking wine) and stir well. Combine cornstarch mixture, butter, and next four ingredients in a large skillet. Bring to boil over medium heat, stirring constantly until butter melts. Add carrot strips, cardamom, pepper, and salt. Cook, tossing gently, until mixture is thoroughly heated. Stir in parsley. Makes 6 servings.

The Doggy Bag

We have all been to a lovely dinner at a favorite restaurant and ordered with eyes bigger than our stomachs. But not to worry—there is always the doggy bag. When there is too much of a good thing left on our plates, we just take the rest home. The next day as we heat up these leftovers and raise the forks to our lips, we relive the delicious meal.

Every lifegiver wants her friends to return home from her hospitality with a yummy take away, a little doggy bag filled with some memory of the time spent together. Sometimes she literally has a gift for each guest, such as a beautifully wrapped candlestick holder, delicate chocolates, or a lovely little picture frame. I like to wrap these gifts and set them on their plates for them to open while I am getting things going in the kitchen. This little gift is also a memento, and every time it is seen, the day or event comes to mind. Remember, what you want to give to each of your guests is a feeling of being loved and cared for. They are special, and their value is what motivates you to do all you do.

And what do your friends remember? The menu? Probably not. The exact topic of conversation? I doubt it. What is evoked is a feeling of warmth, comfort, and love. This is the delightful stuff of lifegiving.

> For the things we have to learn before we can do them, we learn by doing them. Aristotle

Sweet communion

Every time we gather together at the table, we do so much more than just eat. We share the communion of hearts and the comfort of one another's presence. Is it always sweet communion? Well, we do live in a fallen world with less than perfect people on the guest (and host) list. Are there times when everyone leaves, the candles are blown out, the dishes are stacked, and we fall into bed in a heap, with a tear-smeared face? Oh yes. Every lifegiving hostess knows the mental replay of a conversation that went in the wrong direction or a comment that she wished had never passed her own lips. But these are the troubles of everyday life and not the reason to stop living . . . and lifegiving.

So we go to the ultimate Lifegiver. We go to drink from the well of refreshment. We let even the death of high hopes for a successful, unfettered dinner party become material for the compost. We fix our eyes on Jesus and move on. We look ahead to the next time. One attempt at hosting guests that was punctuated by a burned roast or an ill-timed comment will not hold back the lifegiving woman, for practice makes perfect. So she dries her tears, rests awhile, and plans her next gathering.

Many women mistakenly believe that hospitality is a gift for a privileged few. Many are convinced that they do not have this gift, so they hide safely behind this thought. As a matter of fact, this thought has locked the front doors of their homes so that few enter there.

Providing hospitality—just like any other skill we seek to acquire—takes practice to perfect. We may never reach perfection. The soufflé may fall, the kids may knock over the flower vase, or countless other mini-disasters may befall us. But every time we practice, we get better at it, more relaxed, more sure, more able.

So if you are wondering where to begin, begin where you are. Just start! Start small, keep it simple, but get started. The journey of a thousand miles does begin with one small step in the right direction.

The lifegiver is dying to herself, so she takes small failures in her heartfelt attempts in stride. These are lessons in humility! The lifegiver is growing in her confidence in God, so she knows that even her insecurity about hosting others is an opportunity for God to show Himself strong in her weakness. The lifegiving woman is learning to live from the secret place of hiding her life in Christ and doing her work unto the Lord, and her eyes are up, looking to Him for her reward. So when her invitations are not reciprocated, she looks up and says, "I did it as unto You, anyway, Lord." When her preparations are unappreciated, she looks up and says, "You see, Lord." And God, who sees in secret, will generously reward her.

part three

A Few Good
Lifegivers

lifegivers

A Few Good Lifegivers

I have always loved the life stories of women who have overcome serious obstacles to bring forth life. Women who have faced failure, difficulty, and disappointment and yet still press in and press on toward a life well lived. These lifegiving women give us all hope that God can use the compost of our lives, no matter how bad, to miraculously grow in us a beautiful life.

My desire for you is that through this journey you will be inspired to change your world and the world around you by flowing in a lifegiving lifestyle that fills up and overflows. That river will look very different in each of our lives, and the good news is that it's supposed to! Girl, it should look like you . . . with all your personal nuances, your life story, your distinct personality.

I have been in ministry for many years and have had the privilege of hearing the most incredible personal stories. And this I have learned: Each one of us has a story, a story that looks only like *you*. Some of your stories have been laced with everyday pain and disappointment. Others of you may have lived rather uneventful lives, so far from exceptional that lifegiving sounds too good to be true. Still others of you don't even know how to see your life as anything but a sorry mistake. No matter what group you fall into, I have *promising news* for you. All of these roads can lead us to the trusted Lifegiver, Jesus. Some of you know exactly what I mean. Others of you still wonder if God can really do such a work in your life.

Well, go make yourself a cup of tea. Sit down in a comfortable chair and get ready. Prepare to see what lifegiving looks like, lifegiving in the flesh, lifegiving embodied by different women in different settings with very different lives. If God *could* do it for them, if He *could* do it for me, then, dear sister, He *will* do it for you! He is the Lover of your soul, and He is faithful!

> He who began a good work in you will carry it on to
> completion until the day of Christ Jesus.
> (Philippians 1:6)

chapter nine

Phyllis Stanley

lifegivers

Every day should be

distinguished by at

least one particular

act of love.

Johann Kaspar Lavater

It was a beautiful fall morning, complete with a clear blue Colorado sky and sunshine. I was on my way to meet a woman I had heard so much about, and I was late! I parked my Suburban and dashed to the front door of her home. In my haste I dropped my keys, Bible, and notebook just as Phyllis Stanley opened the door to greet me. What a first impression I must have made! Still, I was met with utter warmth and welcome. Already her lovingkindness was pouring out on me as I stood in the doorway. She welcomed me with a warm hug and a smile that flowed from a full, rich heart.

As we walked in, I was taken with her charming home. Her red and white kitchen bustled with women who came for the Bible study Phyllis was teaching. This was a real live party! Phyllis cut me a thick slice of her homemade bread and poured me a cup of black tea with maple syrup. (I would come to enjoy this simple fare time and time again.) There is something about Phyllis that makes women feel safe and accepted. She openly knows how to love. I wondered what her secret was.

Those who know Phyllis have been dramatically affected by the way she brings others into her life. From the first time I talked with her, I remember thinking, "Who *is* this woman?" Even her words felt like a lifegiving embrace. I could not wait to meet her. From that first conversation, I decided that Phyllis Stanley was a woman I wanted to know, *really know*. She had a way about her that was peaceful and caring. I simply could not get enough of this wonderful woman. In the weeks and months that followed, I never wanted to leave when the Bible study was over. For years I had prayed that the Lord would bring an older and wiser woman into my life; a woman who would help me in the journey of motherhood; a woman who would help me be a godly wife to a husband who traveled so often; a woman who would ignite within me a desire to know the Lord on a deeper level. Phyllis was such a woman.

Phyllis and her husband Paul have been married for thirty-eight years, and they have four grown children. They spent thirteen years living in Austria, while Paul served in the military and then with the Navigators establishing the Eastern Europe Navigator ministry. Paul has traveled nearly half of every year since they have been married. When I asked Phyllis how she felt about this, she replied, "I would rather have 'half' a life with Paul than a 'whole' life with anyone else!"

There were many times of loneliness and solitude. Because of these struggles, she learned to reach out beyond her own needs. She was a busy young mother, painfully trying to speak better German and understand the unfamiliar culture. Though she desperately missed her husband, it was this yearning for connection that created something beautiful in her life. Little did she know that the difficulty of those days and the practice of inviting others into her life and home would set the pattern for her life. Phyllis says, "Here I learned what a high privilege it was to love my husband, love my children, and work within my home. It was at this time that I shifted my focus on where 'ministry' happens. I began to see that my home was my platform. I didn't need to go out, because God would bring people in for me to minister the message of Christ."

Phyllis shared the Lord in any way she could with her children's friends and their mothers, with her neighbors and people at the school or her church. It was at this time that she committed herself to a life of hospitality. She learned the beauty of lifegiving by constant practice, and she has elevated it to an art form.

Phyllis lives intentionally and purposefully in her home. She does not let her hours and days slip by wasted. She also does not "draw boundaries," because she has learned to let God control the flow of her schedule. She made that commitment long ago on her knees. It is easy to set a strict schedule and be available or unavailable according to a preset plan. Yet Phyllis prefers to have greater flexibility so she is ready for whatever God may bring her way in a given day. For her, this is Spirit-led living.

She has a home-based business selling bread-making supplies, equipment, and pressure cookers. Half of her garage is a "store." People often stop by to make a purchase or see a demonstration on the grain grinder or find out how to cook potatoes under pressure in just three minutes. Phyllis often says to a customer or friend who stops in, "Why don't you sit for five minutes?" Often many more minutes pass while her visitor is given an opportunity to unburden her heart and sometimes receive prayer.

Whether Phyllis Stanley is preparing a spontaneous breakfast tray graced with scrambled eggs, toast, a little candle, and a small vase with fresh-cut flowers for a house guest; or she is having a luncheon for twenty with beautiful stoneware from Germany, lovely linens, and homebaked goodies; or she is sharing a cup of tea in a special Peter Rabbit teacup with one of her eight grandchildren—whatever she finds to do, she does to bring beauty and loveliness to the lives of others. She says, "I want to create beauty and warmth in my home. I want to lay loving and lovely spiritual foundations in the lives of women." Even in this sweet profession, we see the tender humility with which this lifegiving woman gives her life away.

Phyllis brings others in and loves them with the unconditional love of Jesus Christ. She is the hands and feet of our Savior to so many who need her encouraging words and actions. She is a beautiful, lifegiving woman, and to know her loving ways is to know the loveliness of our Lord.

For more information on Phyllis and her business, go to www.boschcolorado.com.

chapter ten

Cheryl Green

lifegivers

Earth has no

sorrow that

heaven cannot

heal....

Thomas Moore

Aspiring Women often features the stories of everyday women who have overcome enormous setbacks in life and emerged as victorious lifegivers. As a cohost of the show, I have the wonderful opportunity to hear some of these life-changing stories, and I have seen the power of the Savior, the true Giver of all life, unleashed in these women's lives. One woman in particular, Cheryl Green, has an unforgettable story. After reading the story of her hard life and all the ways she had suffered, I wondered how she had lived to tell the tale. Not only has she survived, but she has also become quite an accomplished woman.

Cheryl Green graduated first in her high school class. She went on to receive a full scholarship to Yale University—no small accomplishment! Cheryl was very bright and did well academically at prestigious Yale. What made life difficult for her was not the academic work but physically getting around the campus. Cheryl's bones were fused together while in the womb. In spite of countless surgeries in childhood, she was disabled and had to get around the eighteenth-century campus on crutches. When she arrived, Yale was not handicapped accessible, which posed a great problem for her. Yet after a tumultuous home life growing up, no challenge was too great for Cheryl.

Not only was Cheryl born with a mysterious and debilitating disease, but she was also raised by a mentally ill mother and an alcoholic, depressed father. Her father had a difficult time keeping a job. Between the ages of seven and twelve, Cheryl's family life unraveled. Her father could no longer hold down any job. This led to a nervous breakdown for her mother, and the family was evicted from their home.

One day the unthinkable happened. Cheryl came home from school and found her mother staring blankly into space. While Cheryl was talking on the phone to a friend, her mentally unstable mother

came at her with a knife. As her mother held the knife to her throat,
Cheryl cried out for help. Thank God her sister heard her and came to
her rescue! She wrestled her mother down to the floor and pulled
the knife away from her. From that point on, Cheryl felt very unsafe
with her mother. She felt she had nowhere to turn for help.

Cheryl's mother was diagnosed with schizophrenia. She had a
thought disorder and could not control how and why she acted the
way she did. She suffered from hallucinations and delusions that
caused unbearable pain to the family.

Her parents had long ago burned the bridges of relationships
with extended family members, and there was no place for her family
to turn. They began living in a dangerous park, homeless. She slept
under bushes and trees, anywhere that would somewhat hide her
small body. Every night, Cheryl awoke in terror, thinking that someone
was going to kill the family.

After begging her parents to do something, they put their belong-
ings in a storage facility, which became their new "home." If anyone
found out that they were living in the storage unit, they would be
kicked out and forced to be homeless again. The storage unit was
unbearably hot, without windows or ventilation. Cheryl did her homework by candlelight in the cramped storage space. Most nights she
fell asleep hungry and afraid.

Finally Cheryl's school discovered the family's living condition,
and a social worker stepped in to help. Through the social agency, a
Houston Oilers' player made a charitable gift to the family and offered
to pay for six months of food and shelter for them. This improved life
for a while, giving them a respite from the storm. Then when Cheryl
was in high school, her dad lost his job again and her mother was in
and out of psychiatric wards. The family seemed to hit bottom and

wound up living in a crack house. Cheryl woke up one morning and decided that was the day she would take her own life. Life was just not getting any better.

Cheryl had a clear plan to overdose on some of her mother's pills that day, but a strange thing happened. It was a simple act, but one that made the difference between life and death for Cheryl. At school that day, a popular girl came and sat next to Cheryl. The girl told Cheryl she looked like she needed a friend. Though the girl was a Christian, she did not share Christ with Cheryl that day—not with words anyway.

The girl invited Cheryl to join her youth group at the bowling alley, and then she invited her over to her house. For the next two to three weeks, this family gave life to Cheryl. No one preached at her; they just reached out to her. Finally Cheryl asked her new friend, "How do you know God loves you?" After a wonderful discussion, Cheryl met Christ that day! Little did this kind girl know that her gift of life to Cheryl would keep on giving—to more people than her friend could have ever known!

Cheryl's challenges at Yale were nothing compared to the agony of her early years. She wanted to study at Yale, yet to do so meant something had to be done on campus. She decided to bring a lawsuit against Yale University, claiming their noncompliance with the Americans with Disabilities Act. It was a bold but successful move that attracted the attention of Washington and of Senator Bob Dole in particular. Senator Dole was a strong proponent of the ADA and thought Cheryl's case was worth his support. The University responded and asked Cheryl if she would give them a year to make the campus accessible. Cheryl agreed, and in the meantime she went to work as an intern with Senator Dole. Things were looking up for Cheryl. She says, "God whispered in my ear continuously. . . . Whenever I wanted to give up, the day wouldn't turn out quite as bad as I thought it might."

Last year Cheryl published her first book, *Child of Promise*. The theme of the book is something she had begun to experience personally: "Earth has no sorrow that heaven cannot heal." Though her father has passed away, her mother still suffers with mental illness. Cheryl has come to accept that some experiences are to be managed and may never change. She says, "We want answers for every problem we face, but sometimes there just aren't answers, and often the answers we receive aren't the ones we want. We have to learn to be at peace with that." The countless difficulties this woman has faced have molded her into an incredible lifegiving woman of strength and beauty. Cheryl says, "My one problem is I might smile too much."

Cheryl earned advanced degrees in psychology, has been a professor of psychology, has worked with Senator Dole's foundation for people with disabilities, has helped implement the ADA by training businesses in compliance issues, and has served on numerous boards and foundations to direct funds to groups that help people with disabilities. Cheryl has a heart to help individuals, one at a time.

Cheryl moved back to Dallas so that she could live near her mother. Cheryl's mom is fifty-eight, and it is a wonder that she is alive. Her severe mental problems are extremely rare. Although Cheryl feels helpless and frustrated at times, she holds onto God in faith. She says that she is like the persistent widow, and she will not stop pestering the Lord on behalf of her mother! Cheryl is working on several other books that will address living a life of faith in light of mental and physical disabilities. She wants to give hope to others through her story.

Though Cheryl believes her "thorn in the flesh" is her own physical disability, she does not ask for her own healing anymore. Her one request for healing is for her mother. It is with this request that Cheryl often looks to the Lord. And it is easy to see that she looks to Him often, because His reflection shines brightly on Cheryl's countenance.

chapter eleven

Melinda Wallace

lifegivers

Wherever there
is a human being
there is a chance
for kindness.

Seneca

Through a longtime friend, Seth Barns, I met a lifegiving dynamo named Melinda Wallace. It all began at one of my favorite restaurants south of Denver, The Little Stone Church. We were catching up on what was happening with Seth's busy family and their ever-expanding ministry, Adventures in Missions. God was doing many exciting things through their work. Seth is a rational sort of guy, so it is always fun to hear him tell stories that have taken even him out of his comfort zone.

As the evening continued, Seth asked me about the book I was writing. What a question to ask an author! I told him all about my book . . . for hours! I described the beauty of a lifegiving woman, her drive, her passion, the mystery of how she takes the dead places of life and finds God's purpose. This woman is a risk taker, a people-focused person, a lover of God to the end, I said.

Seth was quiet for a moment and then ventured, "Tammy, I have someone for you to meet. Her name is Melinda Wallace." He told me that Melinda has given her life away in the desperate places of this world where people are dying daily. He said that some even call her the young Mother Teresa.

Well, to say he got my attention is an understatement. I wanted to meet this woman! I wanted to know why a beautiful, young, single, educated woman would give up all the comforts of this world to go and serve people who have so little of this world. At the end of our dinner, Seth handed me Melinda's business card. I can still remember the words at the top of her card: "What you and I do with our lives determines whether heaven or hell increases in occupation." Already, this woman had inspired me.

Several weeks later I spoke with Melinda. She embodies the picture of what a strong lifegiving woman looks like. She boldly goes where I would be terrified to go. I really liked this lady. She departs from what is conventional and reaches out with what is supernatural. If you ask her about her work, she tells you she is the richer one for it. Melinda shared, "As we search for His presence in the poverty and pain, we discover there is no place on earth His love cannot penetrate. He has come to search for the lost, comfort the afflicted, and defend the rights of the poor and needy."

Melinda has racked up more than seventy-five thousand air miles per year for the last fifteen years, visiting and giving life to children all over the globe. Her mission is to touch the lives of these precious children trapped in poverty. These little ones live in Mozambique, Bosnia, Calcutta, and the Sudan. They live in thatched huts, unstable little hovels that were paid for with scarce funds and are at risk of being washed away by each passing storm.

She does not stand on the outside of poverty and gingerly peek in. She goes into the heart of the dumps in impoverished cities and refugee camps. As the crowds gather, she sees each individual for who he or she is: a human being created in the image of God, just like her. She reaches down to pray for the people who are lying despondent in the garbage. Here—even and especially here—the Spirit of the Lord manifests Himself. Before long, a church service starts. She draws the people together and leads them in celebration and worship to the Lord. A local pastor who accompanies her starts preaching, and she and the people begin to dance in worship—right there on top of the garbage!

Melinda has walked along land-mined paths and has seen starvation swallow up thirty thousand lives a day. She has been surrounded by angry mobs intent on killing her and has had Uzi guns and machetes waved in her face. Death has looked her in the eye. Melinda has no illusions about living in anything other than a severely depraved world. She has willingly subjected herself to mosquitoes that can kill with one bite and has braced herself to hear the frantic sobs of parents who shove their babies into her hands, hoping she will transport their children to a better place. She faces such suffering because she is convinced that is what Jesus would do. She knows Him as Isaiah 53 portrays Him—a Man of Sorrows who is well acquainted with grief.

Melinda feels equally passionate about challenging Christians in prosperous nations to understand and help the plight of the desperately poor around the world. She realizes this facet of her ministry may not always be popular, but she feels compelled to bring these needs into the comfortable living rooms of the Western world. A close friend once said, "Melinda comforts the afflicted and afflicts the comfortable."

"Though it doesn't sound like a pleasant assignment, if it is my mission, I have everyone's best intentions at heart," Melinda says. "It is very possible that our attempts at making life more comfortable might actually be insulating us from the very life God wants us to enter into. You see, light is meant to dispel darkness, so if we are avoiding the gaping open wounds of humanity, we are perverting the purpose of His light. Darkness can only be expelled by light, and God's true children are to be carriers, not insulators, of His light."

She asks us, "Would you cry over what breaks God's heart? Will you face the raw pain of our world and move toward it rather than away from it? Will you be His hands and heart where the darkness is obliterating the light?"

Melinda has felt this intense burden for the poor and oppressed for many years. When she was in junior high, she began reading the Bible. The passages that relate to the poor, oppressed, and distressed were like flashing red lights in her mind. She could not help but notice them. It took her a while to figure out that others in the church did not seem to be reading these passages with the same passionate response. Eventually, it became clear to Melinda that if the Holy Spirit gave her this strong burden, then she was responsible for acting on that conviction. She believes that if God is concerned about the poor, then He must want us to be concerned too. It is just that simple.

Melinda urges Christians blessed with comfort to be uncomfortable for at least a season. She says it takes a minimum of two weeks in a foreign country, living among the distressed, to "enter into" their sufferings. Even when Christians cannot go, she urges them to help, even in small outreach efforts. She says, "My New Zealand home group sent a shoe box full of 69-cent bouncy balls to me for the children in Mozambique. As I described to them the joy that just one of those balls brought to a boy named Adelso, they realized they had no excuse for not reaching beyond their borders."

In the days following September 11th, Melinda was stranded overseas. Her mind raced, trying to find answers and insight into the horrible event. "As I sought God for answers about the terrorist attacks in New York, I was like Ransom in C. S. Lewis's *Perelandra*, who cried out, 'God, why don't you do something?' The answer I heard is His answer to me: 'Ransom, you are what I'm doing!'"

We, too, are what He is doing.

For more information on Melinda and her ministry, go to www.zest.faithweb.com.

chapter twelve

Debi Godsey

lifegivers

> The Lord is close to the
>
> brokenhearted,
>
> and he saves those
>
> whose spirits have been
>
> crushed.
>
> *Psalm 34:18* (NCV)

Jesus, the Healer of broken hearts

As a little girl, Debi Godsey was just like me in many ways. She cherished the thought of a pretty dress to wear, imagined the wonder of a new baby doll, and danced freely to the magic of a sweet melody. Like me, she was a little girl who yearned to belong and who longed to be loved. Yet early in her life, her story unfolded quite differently than mine.

Yes, Debi and I shared many longings, but she was met with unmitigated horror, experiences that would chill your heart to imagine. At a tender age, she knew deep rejection, exploitation, violence, and resulting shame. Being loved was only a fairy tale in the stories she read. Her sense of "normal" was a living hell.

Ever since Debi can remember, her family life was ransacked by abuse on every level. All her fingers and several ribs had been broken in fits of rage against her. She knew the devastatingly painful effects of concussions, large portions of her hair being pulled out, deep bruises fresh each morning, and teeth smashed and broken. On a regular basis she was terrorized by sexual abuse from family members. All innocence was violently, purposefully stolen.

Debi remembers one time the abuse was so horrific that she felt her heart would never heal. As she frantically ran into the woods behind her house, she recalled hearing about a good Mother Earth. She wondered if this Mother Earth could heal her broken heart. With tears flowing down her face, she unbuttoned her shirt and pressed her heart on the cold, hard ground, pleading with some spirit, some god out there, to rescue her from this living hell. The one god she knew she would never trust was the God of the Bible, for her abusers "carried around Bibles under their arms, using God as a weapon." How could God really love her if He allowed such abuse?

But even then, her heavenly Father was pursuing her.

The cycle of abuse continued into her adult relationships. She ended up in relationship after relationship that was filled with violence and cruelty. At one very low point, she found herself locked in a garage with the windows boarded up, naked, with no way out. The man who had done this to her said it was his way of keeping her from running. Finally she escaped, and to survive she began a life of prostitution. Prostitution gave her a sense of control, and the drugs and alcohol numbed the shame and anguish.

By the time she was thirty-two, Debi had an eleven-year-old daughter, she was living with a man, and her second marriage was ending in divorce. She said, "I was hopeless and desperate. I had no place to turn, so I planned how I would end my life and get out of this torturous pain once and for all."

God heard Debi's cries, and He already had a plan for her magnificent rescue. Debi was soon to see what the Creator of the universe could do with the horrible compost of her life. It was not *in spite of* the lifelessness of her existence but rather *because of* it that Jesus would heal her heart and bring glory to Himself.

Ten days before her divorce was final, her husband's old "drinking buddy" talked to him about trying to save the marriage. He told him that he would be praying for both of them and invited them to a Family Life "Weekend to Remember" marriage event. This really bothered Debi's husband. He wondered what on earth had happened to his buddy. He had been conspicuously absent from the bars for a long time. Perhaps he had become a religious crazy man or something. Yet he listened, and in his friend's words, he heard hope. His friend told him that he would be really angry with him if he did not at least try before they gave up on their marriage. So they both reluctantly agreed to go, entirely bent on continuing with the divorce.

That night both Debi and Tim heard for the very first time that

God loved them and had created them for a wonderful purpose. They also heard that God was the Creator of marriage and that He had a purpose and plan for their marriage. At that point, Debi knew she was a dying woman grasping at straws. If something did not significantly change in her life, she planned to kill herself.

At the end of the evening, Dennis Rainey challenged those who wanted to ask Christ into their lives and start fresh with their hearts and their marriages to raise their hands. Not wanting Tim to see that she was raising her hand, she raised it on the opposite side of where Tim was sitting. Unbeknownst to her, Tim was doing the exact same thing!

Debi went up to talk to Dennis and told him that she was a woman who had lost all hope. She told him about her failed marriages and the abuse she suffered as a child. Dennis looked right at her and replied, "Well, I guess you have some forgiveness issues to resolve . . . starting with your husband." Debi thought, *Me, forgive?! He is the one who needs to ask me for forgiveness!* But Dennis went on to tell her that forgiving those who had so terribly hurt her was the only way through the pain.

That night as they left, Debi and Tim fought to be the first to ask the other for forgiveness. They had agreed to try again, with the help of Christ, to heal the areas of their marriage that they had destroyed. Immediately their lives started to change. The drinking, the drugs, and the sexual breaches in their relationship no longer brought any satisfaction. They began to pray together. Jesus was teaching them how to love one another and how to forgive one another. He was showing Debi that there was a way out of her hopelessness, out of feeling trapped, and out of her bitter self-hatred. He was teaching her that He could be trusted, even though many who had hidden behind His name had hurt her deeply.

lifegivers

debi godsey

"You know, I don't know why they used God's name to do the things they did," Debi said. "But I can tell you that that is not who Jesus is. No, *Jesus is the Healer of broken hearts*. He is the heart full of the love you are looking for. . . . You will never find it in the arms of a man, in the needle filled with drugs, or a glass of liquor to help you forget. You will only find meaning and worth in the person of Jesus Christ. He is the One who created in you a vacuum that only He can fill. The pain and shame can be gone—you can be free from it. There is another way."

Debi and Tim now live their lives to breathe hope into others who feel hopeless. They have opened their home to about fifteen homeless people—former drug addicts, unemployed people, alcoholics, outcast children, even a patient on kidney dialysis. They share with these hurting people that Christ is the answer. They are not afraid to walk the sometimes long road of recovery with hard-core addicts. Because of their background, they can speak with authority about the hope and transforming power of Jesus Christ. Together they reach out to the hopeless, the sinners, the outcasts of society—exactly those whom Christ came to seek and save.

For more information on Family Life Marriage conferences, go to www.familylife.com.

epilogue

Meet the Ultimate Lifegiver

ultimate

The great Easter truth is not
that we are to live newly after
death, but that we are to be
new here and now by the
power of the resurrection.

Phillip Brooks

Dear friend, can you relate to one of these lifegivers' stories? Maybe you have secretly suffered under the crush of abuse like Debi did, or you've known depression as an unwelcome companion. Have you struggled with addiction, not knowing how to set your foot on new, higher ground? Perhaps you have faced rejection and shame, like Cheryl did. Or you may have grown up in a Christian home but stepped outside of fellowship with Christ, like Phyllis did as a young woman. Is the Lord nudging your heart with a specific burden for ministry, as Melinda felt, yet you haven't known how to respond?

The hope that these women found can be your hope too. It is the hope that is found in a personal relationship with the Lord Jesus Christ. Trying to be good and striving to feel and act better does not win God's approval. No. He stands right now, with wide-open arms, ready to receive you just as you are. Right now, even if you are so low you wonder if you will see the light of day again. Right now, even if you feel gripped by depression or addiction. Right now, Christ is looking at you with unfathomable love in His eyes.

The Bible, which is God's love letter to us, says that His love is so deep, so wide, and so high that it is beyond our ability to comprehend. He revealed that love in the life of Jesus Christ.

When Jesus Christ came to earth, He willingly left the side of the Father in heaven and took on the form of a man. He was perfect in every way, because He was and is God, yet He took on human flesh. *Why? Who would ever leave comfort for discomfort? Who would suffer such mockery, rejection, abuse, and finally death at the hands of mere people if He were indeed God?*

Friend, only God would do it, and only God could do it. And He did it for you. A sacrifice had to be made for our sin, to deliver us from the grip of our addictions, the depth of our willfulness, the prison of our unforgiveness toward others for their sins against us. A price had to be paid, and God Himself stepped in and paid it. Having been cherished with a love like that, my dear friend, what else can we do but love Him with our lives in return?

Have you ever received His forgiveness? Will you confess to Christ your wrongdoing and receive the forgiveness that is yours? Will you forgive those who have hurt you so deeply, just as Christ has forgiven you? Dear one, if you have never received His life, today you can move from spiritual death to spiritual life through Christ. You can be the beautiful lifegiving woman you were created to be.

Will you pray this prayer with me?

> Father in heaven, I have sinned. I have been willfully disobedient. I confess the sins that have kept me in bondage all of my life. (Feel free to share with the Lord specific sins that come to mind.) Thank You for forgiving me. Thank You that Christ's blood was shed for my forgiveness. Father, I receive Your forgiveness now and choose to forgive myself.
> Father, in Jesus' name, I release the people who have hurt me. As You have forgiven me, so I forgive them with Your help and grace. (Feel free to list their names.)
> Father, I receive the Holy Spirit right now. Thank You that You promised that You will never leave me or forsake me. Thank You that I will live eternally with You. Help me to live the rest of my days on earth serving others and sharing Your lifegiving touch. Just as I have received Your life through Christ, help me live as the lifegiving woman You created me to be. Help me to trust that You can and will produce life out of the compost of my life. Help

me faithfully plant seeds in the lives of others. Help
me make my home a place of beauty and loving hospitality.
Lead me in Your paths, the right paths, all the days
of my life. In Jesus' name I pray, Amen.

Congratulations, dear friend! Your newfound life has begun. You
are indeed the beautiful lifegiving woman God has created you to be.

Now start simply in your relationship with your loving Jesus . . .
and yes, simply start. I'll see you along the way!

endnotes

1. Mother Teresa, *No Greater Love* (Novato, CA: New World Library, 1997), 137–138.

2. Danielle Crittenden, *What Our Mothers Didn't Tell Us* (New York: Touchstone, 1999), 82.

3. Dietrich Bonhoeffer, *The Cost of Discipleship* (New York: Macmillan, 1959), 79.

4. Alexandra Stoddard, *Living a Beautiful Life* (New York: Avon, 1986), 4.

Family

Family Life

www.familylife.com
1-800-FL-TODAY

This excellent site gives timely information about the Family Life marriage conferences and is also a superb resource on marriage and family life. It includes resources for making your remarriage work and having a successful blended family, as well as tremendous support for the single parent.

Seasons of a Woman's Life by Lois Evans (Moody Press)

Lois Evans is married to Dr. Tony Evans, senior pastor of Oak Cliff Bible Fellowship in Dallas. This book is a wonderful encouragement for women who are afraid that they may never be done with dirty diapers and carpool duty. With wisdom and personal stories, Lois helps women understand that we will eventually have all God has planned for us—just not all at once!

What is a Family? by Edith Schaeffer (Baker Books)

This classic book provides insight into healthy and whole family life. Through personal testimonies of triumphs and failures, Edith describes the sweeping landscape of family life lived out in the mundane day-to-day activities as well as special celebrations.

What to Do Until Love Finds You: Getting Ready for Mr. Right by Michelle McKinney Hammond (Harvest House Publishers)

Michelle asks, "Are you ready to be found? Are you ready to leave the single life behind?" She draws a road map with humorous and insightful illustrations leading women through the sometimes rough terrain of single life.

The Vision Forum, Inc.

www.visionforum.com

1-800-440-0022 to request a catalog

The Vision Forum web site explains the ministry's purpose to rebuild Christian family culture. Though Vision Forum promotes homeschooling, which is only one of many school options for families today, this ministry provides helpful materials for instilling time-honored family values in your children. The *Beautiful Girlhood Collection* offers books such as *Beautiful Girlhood, What's a Girl to Do?, Wives of the Signers,* and inspiring stories on the lives of Priscilla Mullins (a Pilgrim), Nan Harper (who sailed on the Titanic), Dolley Madison, and Sacajawea. The Girlhood collection also includes dolls, clothes, and cookery for girls. *The All-American Boys Adventure Catalog* is an inspiring collection of costumes, tools, books, toys, and memorabilia for boys of all ages.

Hospitality

Better Homes and Gardens

www.bhg.com

Some of the best and easiest ideas for creating a beautiful home and garden and for creating wonderful memories with your children are found here—not to mention many of my *best* recipes!

www.eat.epicurious.com

A wonderful web site that offers excellent recipes and presentations.

Barefoot Contessa Parties! by Ina Garten (Clarkson N. Potter)

Ideas and recipes for easy parties that are really fun. If you buy *one* book on how to cook for a wonderful party, this is it. The recipes are real (as in you actually *know* what the ingredients are and can find them in a normal grocery store). The book is filled with wonderful pictures—and what's a cookbook without pictures to inspire you? You will love this book!

Emily Post's Entertaining by Peggy Post (Harper Perennial)

A fun book with how-to's and know-how's for entertaining, setting a table, sending out invitations, how to be a good hostess, how to keep a conversation going, and more.

In The Kennedy Style by Letitia Baldridge (Doubleday)

For those who want a peek into White House entertaining, this book is captivating. We may never dwell in the White House, but we can glean from Jackie's enduring style.

Home

BALLARD DESIGNS

www.ballarddesigns.com
1-800-367-2775

An interior design magazine with many good ideas to copy! I have purchased many items from their catalog and have been pleased with the quality.

Living a Beautiful Life (Avon Books), *Feeling at Home* (William Morrow & Company), and *Creating a Beautiful Home* (Avon Books) by Alexandra Stoddard

Add elegance, order, beauty, and joy to every day of your life. These books are a true delight to read and a wonderfully inspiring experience. Alexandra Stoddard provides timeless insights for making a house a home.

www.Frugal-Moms.com

This site gives you great, lifegiving ideas on a budget. I've been very impressed with the ideas and philosophy of this site. Their mission to help women enjoy life *now*—not later when our situations are different—is an inspirational, empowering message.

www.myhouseandgarden.com

Fantastic web site filled with ideas for hospitality, holiday celebrations, gardening, home décor, and so very much more! Their site includes a link to the one-hundred top cooking sites . . . and even tells how to host a traditional afternoon tea.

Friendship

Can I Afford Time for Friendships? by Stormie Omartian, Ruth Senter, and Colleen Evans (Bethany House)

Food for thought for all friends. These women discuss the unmentionables in friendship—the effort and time it takes to be a friend, how we feel when someone moves out of our life, and how to deal with a critical heart. The beauty of friendship is brought forth in this book.

Celebrating Friendship by Judith Couchman (Zondervan)

Designed for group study, *Celebrating Friendship* is one of Women of Faith's six-week, interactive Bible studies. This study has six sessions: "Wanted: A Few Good Women," "Nobody's Just Like You," "Thank God!," "Hugs and a Good, Swift Kick," "Putting Your Feet to the Fire," "Friendship Flops and Fizzles," and "Come On, Get Happy!" For the sake of your health, the sake of your sanity, the sake of your soul, you've gotta have friends.

The Twelve Teas of Friendship by Emilie Barnes (Harvest House Publishers)

We'll have tea on the veranda today, where white wicker, floral chintz, and lace cloths set a gracious mood amidst the climbing roses. Welcome to Emilie's new collection of monthly teatime celebrations, brimming with fresh recipes, decorating tips, and fun ideas for creating a cozy atmosphere.

Coffee Cup Friendship & Cheesecake Fun by Becky Freeman (Harvest House Publishers)

Celebrate life as you spend time with treasured friends, pause to think and laugh aloud, and invest in relationships—the only things we carry into eternity! In this heartwarming volume, Freeman weaves inspiring quotes and real-life experiences into a tapestry of love and laughter. Sprinkled throughout is a collection of mouthwatering recipes.

Lemonade Laughter and Laid-Back Joy by Becky Freeman (Harvest House Publishers)

Does your life run on fast-forward? Do your friends and family wonder why you talk in rapid-fire mode? Sit back and take a long, cool drink from this glass of contentment. Freeman's laugh-out-loud stories and encouraging insights guide you down a less hurried, less worried road, following the laid-back lifestyle of Jesus.

The Blessing Of Friendship by Karla Dornacher (J. Countryman)

When Karla Dornacher began drawing as a child, she didn't take it seriously—until she became a Christian and decided to use her artistic talents to glorify God. Her newest book celebrates one of God's most precious gifts—friendship. Winsome illustrations, heartwarming reflections, Scripture verses, and journaling space encourage you to record special moments shared with friends.

Your Gift of Friendship: Selections from Thank You for Being A Friend by Jill Briscoe (Moody Press)

When you can't be there to give your friend a hug, this touching gift book is the next best thing! Inspiring Scripture, luminous pastel photographs, simple expressions of friendship, and Briscoe's warm personal stories will embrace your companion with love, encouragement, and beautiful reminders of God's grace.

Treasured Friends: Finding and Keeping True Friendships by Ann Hibbard (Baker Books)

Most women long for deep, intimate friendships. But how do we find—and keep—true friends who will encourage us, motivate us, and bring us closer to God? With warmth and honesty, Hibbard encourages believers along the path to meaningful community and accountability in Christ.

The Friendships of Women by Dee Brestin

A classic book on friendship. It will transform the way you think of your friends and the value of friendships.

The Inner Life

You Are My Hiding Place by Amy Carmichael (Bethany House)

When you want to go deep with the Lord, this little devotional will show you the path. Missionary Amy Carmichael lived a life of true sacrifice and love. Enter into her secret place with the Lord. You will be inspired and encouraged to be the lifegiving woman God created you to be.

Secrets of the Secret Place and *The Fire of God's Love* by Bob Sorge (Oasis House)

These two books give you life-changing sparks to ignite your personal time with God and your passion to know and understand His love. These books show how God uses the compost of our lives and sets us free to live. These books have changed my perspective on God in big and powerful ways.

My All for Him by Basilea Schlink (Bethany House)

Basilea Schlink led the Evangelical Sisterhood of Mary, dedicated to working and praying for the spiritual enrichment of others. This book is a collection of messages originally written in German. Each meditation conveys the challenging aspects of living a life of abiding in Christ.

The Pursuit of God by A. W. Tozer (Christian Publications)

Tozer is considered a twentieth-century prophet. He was a Chicago pastor who ministered to hundreds of thousands through preaching and writing. This book is one of many works by Tozer that knock us out of mediocrity to recenter our lives on Christ.

Loving Jesus by Mother Teresa (Servant Publications)

Mother Teresa founded the Missionaries of Charity, ministering among the destitute and dying in India. In this book, her heart shines through in chapters like "Loving People, Not Things," "The Hands and Feet of Jesus," "God's Love in Action," and "Love Changes Hearts."

My Utmost For His Highest by Oswald Chambers

This is truly *the* devotional classic for the Christian life. If you have never experienced these daily readings, buy this book today and start tomorrow! Chambers' insights will change your life.

Prayer Portions by Sylvia Gunter

Available through The Father's Business, P.O. Box 888014, Atlanta, GA 30356.

Reams of practical guides containing Scripture prayers for your home, family, business, and ministry, compiled by Sylvia Gunter and available through The Father's Business. These are resources you will use and share again and again.

www.Crosswalk.com

This is an online clearinghouse of values-based and Christian resources for daily living.

Adoption

HOLT INTERNATIONAL SERVICES WWW.HOLTINTT.ORG

P.O. Box 2880
Eugene, OR 97402
1-541-687-2202

This is the Christian adoption agency through which we adopted Tatiana, and as far as I am concerned, they are the best. If they cannot help you with the adoption of a child, they can send you to the right place. Go ahead and give them a call—adoption is a beautiful way to build a family!

Holt's Mission statement: "Thousands of children around the world face the day alone. For reasons beyond their control, they no longer have families to nurture them and give them hope for tomorrow. Circumstances put others in danger of losing their families forever. Holt International Children's Services is dedicated to carrying out God's plan for every child to have a permanent, loving home through family preservation, in-country adoption, and international adoption."

BETHANY CHRISTIAN SERVICES

www.bethany.org
1-800-BETHANY

Bethany's Mission statement: "Bethany Christian Services manifests the love and compassion of Jesus Christ by protecting and enhancing the lives of children and families through quality social services." Bethany has offices in various states across the nation and offers a wide variety of services to birth parents and adoptive parents for both domestic and foreign adoption.

If you are considering domestic adoption, you may contact Bethany through their contact information listed above. A woman in a crisis pregnancy who is considering adoption can contact Bethany at 1-800-BETHANY for loving support and assistance.

If you are interested in contacting Tammy to speak or would like to send her a personal testimony on lifegiving, please contact her at lifegivingwomen@netscape.net.

About the Authors

Tammy Maltby is co-host of Total Living Network's *Aspiring Women*. Through her nationally televised segments and her writing and speaking she mentors women in the lifegiving lifestyle. Her life-altering message of hope and freedom springs from the confidence that God Himself uses the dead places of our lives to create beauty. Tammy lives near the Rocky Mountains of Colorado with her husband, Butch, and their four children, two of whom they have adopted internationally.

Tamra Farah is former executive director of crisis pregnancy centers in San Diego, California and Columbus, Ohio and is a freelance writer and homemaker, and has served in the women's ministry at her church in Colorado Springs, Colorado. She and her husband, Barry, lead The Barnabas Center, which provides leadership symposiums for emerging Christian leaders. Tamra has been instrumental in the development and support of local charities, mentor programs, and charter schools. She and Barry have two children.

SINCE 1894, Moody Publishers has been dedicated to equip and motivate people to advance the cause of Christ by publishing evangelical Christian literature and other media for all ages, around the world. Because we are a ministry of the Moody Bible Institute of Chicago, a portion of the proceeds from the sale of this book go to train the next generation of Christian leaders.

If we may serve you in any way in your spiritual journey toward understanding Christ and the Christian life, please contact us at www.moodypublishers.com.

"All Scripture is God-breathed and is useful for teaching, rebuking, correcting and training in righteousness, so that the man of God may be thoroughly equipped for every good work."
—2 TIMOTHY 3:16, 17

MOODY
PUBLISHERS

THE NAME YOU CAN TRUST®

Discover How to Practice...
The Art of Lifegiving

ISBN: 0-8024-1361-7

Lifegiving is much more than an idea—it's a breathtaking, beautiful way to live and love.

Written as a companion journal to the book *Lifegiving*, this workbook will help you discover how to practice the art of lifegiving. Here you will search the Scriptures, reflect on the promises of God, the supreme Lifegiver, and explore what may be blocking you from giving to others. There are also some fun, easy ideas for entertaining and cooking—the emphasis being on loving and serving those around you.

As you learn to practice lifegiving in your friendships, your family, and your home, you'll find the wonderful freedom and joy that comes from giving your life away.

MOODY
PUBLISHERS

THE NAME YOU CAN TRUST.

1-800-678-6928 www.MoodyPublishers.org

LIFEGIVING TEAM

ACQUIRING EDITOR:
Elsa Mazon

COPY EDITOR & INTERIOR DESIGN:
The Livingstone Corporation

BACK COVER COPY:
Paige Drygas, The Livingstone Corporation

COVER DESIGN:
Journey Group

PRINTING AND BINDING:
Color House Graphics Inc.

The typeface for the text of this book is
ITC Cheltenham